Andrei Sakharov
and **human rights**

Council of Europe Publishing

The opinions expressed in this work are the responsibility of the author(s) and do not necessarily reflect the official policy of the Council of Europe.

All rights reserved. No part of this publication may be translated, reproduced or transmitted, in any form or by any means, electronic (CD-Rom, Internet, etc.) or mechanical, including photocopying, recording or any information storage or retrieval system, without prior permission in writing from the Public Information Division, Directorate of Communication (F-67075 Strasbourg Cedex or publishing@coe.int).

Cover photo: Sakharov at the General Meeting of the Academy of Sciences, Moscow, 27 December 1988. © L. Sherstennikov 1988.
Back cover photo: Sakharov working at home, Moscow, winter 1987. © Yuri Rost, 1987.
Cover design: Documents and Publications Production Department (SPDP),
Council of Europe
Layout: Jouve, Paris

Council of Europe Publishing
F-67075 Strasbourg Cedex
http://book.coe.int

ISBN 978-92-871-6947-1
© Council of Europe, December 2010
Printed at the Council of Europe

Contents

Acknowledgements 6
Foreword 7
Editor's note 9
Introduction 11
    Nobel presentation speech 11

I. Autobiography 19
    An autobiographical note 19
    Exile in Gorky 24
    Return to Moscow 28

II. Andrei Sakharov's vision and world view 33
    Prologue to *My Country and the World* 33
    Reflections on Progress, Co-existence and Intellectual Freedom 35
    Postscript to Memorandum 45
    Interview with Olle Stenholm 50
    Nobel lecture: Peace, progress, human rights 53
    Open letter to the President of the Academy of Sciences 56
    Danger of thermonuclear war 61
    The inevitability of perestroika 61
    Concluding statement to the First Congress of People's Deputies 74

III. Human rights activities 79

The responsibility of scientists 80
Eastern Europe 85
The human rights movement in the USSR 87
A Chronicle of Current Events 90
The Initiative Group for the Defence of Human Rights 92
The Moscow Human Rights Committee 94
The Memorial Society 99
Appeals and action 101
Rehabilitation of Stalin 102
Prisoners of conscience and political prisoners 105
Political trials and the rule of law 111
Abolition of the death penalty 118
Protection of the environment 124
International responsibility for human rights 128

IV. In tribute 131

Sergei Kovalev:
Andrei Dmitrievich Sakharov: Meeting the demands of reason 131

Valentin Turchin: My memory of Andrei Dmitrievich Sakharov 139

Valery Chalidze:
Andrei Sakharov and the Russian intelligentsia 141

Pavel Litvinov: In search of dialogue 146

Yuri Orlov 151

Interview with President Mikhail Gorbachev 155
President Boris Yeltsin 162
President Dmitry Medvedev 163
Efrem Yankelevich: Sakharov's alternatives 163
Václav Havel: Preface to the *Collected Works of Andrei Sakharov* 169
Adam Michnik: Sakharov from a Polish perspective 171
Thomas Hammarberg: The relevance of Andrei Sakharov's example and message on human rights in today's world 174

Appendix 1
Andrei Sakharov – A chronology 181

Appendix 2
Bibliography 191

Acknowledgements

The Commissioner wishes to thank Elena Bonner, Valery Chalidze, Václav Havel, Izvestiya, Edward Kline, Sergei Kovalev, Adam Michnik, Yuri Orlov, Yuri Rost, Tanya Turchin, Random House Inc., The Nobel Foundation, and Vremya for their permission to use texts in this book.

He also thanks the Andrei Sakharov Archive, Elena Bonner, ITAR-TASS, Pavel Litvinov, Yuri Rost, L. Sherstennikov, Hedrick Smith, R. Sobol, Radii Tsimerinov, and I. Zarembo for permitting use of the photographs included in the book.

Foreword

Autocratic rulers seek to prevent any form of criticism. They want silence. Standing up for human rights requires breaking this silence and exposing the facts as they are. Even in the most repressive societies there have been individuals who have resisted injustice and spoken out with a principled critique of society, often against the prevailing spirit of their times and at great personal cost – thereby giving courage to others. Andrei Dmitrievich Sakharov, the eminent Russian physicist and Nobel peace laureate, was such a man and one of the great human rights champions of our age.

These readings set out to capture the significance of Andrei Sakharov for Europe today. The circumstances in which Sakharov lived were, of course, different – the Second World War, followed by the Cold War, a world divided into East and West, one where competing powers brought immense suffering to people throughout the world, and where ideological rivalries shaped understandings of human rights in ways far removed from their original spirit and intent.

Sakharov understood the deeper significance of human rights and their centrality for a peaceful and just world. Much has changed in the two decades since his death, but many problems Sakharov confronted remain: unaccountable regimes and institutions; politicised trials; inhumane prison conditions; the retention of the death penalty; curbs on freedoms of association and assembly; denial of freedom of expression and the free exchange of information and ideas; and the suppression of those who speak out.

We have sought to select readings which resonate today and to structure them so that they make up a coherent whole. The presentation speech made in Oslo in December 1975, when Sakharov received the Nobel Peace Prize, forms the introduction both to Sakharov and to this publication. An autobiographical section follows. Subsequent sections draw from Sakharov's writings to cast light on his vision, on his ideas and on his actions to defend human rights. Commentary has been kept to a minimum to allow Sakharov to speak in his own words. The publication ends with tributes to Sakharov, which enrich our understanding of this remarkable man, of his courage, and of his efforts to bring about a more humane, peaceful world.

I would like to thank Margo Picken for having edited this publication and Edward Kline, President of the Andrei Sakharov Foundation in the USA, for his advice in the process. I also thank Elena Bonner for her generosity in making available so much material written by her husband, as well as the staff of the Andrei Sakharov Archive (Bela Koval, Ekaterina Shikhanovich, and Elena Saveleva) and the Andrei Sakharov Centre in Moscow, which prepared the Russian version.

Thomas Hammarberg
Council of Europe Commissioner for Human Rights

Editor's note

Most of the readings in this publication are taken from existing publications of Andrei Sakharov's writings in English, which are now sadly out of print. In some cases, translations have been slightly modified to reflect more clearly the original Russian text or to improve readability.

Margo Picken

I was once asked whether it was easy to live with a genius. The question was unexpected for me. I simply loved Andrei Sakharov, although I understood, of course, that I was the companion of a man of extraordinary intellectual courage, a good and honest man, who was definite and unerring in his moral decisions and who lived according to them.

Elena "Lusia" Bonner[1]

Introduction

Nobel presentation speech by Aase Lionnaes, Chairman of the Nobel Committee of the Norwegian Storting[2]

Your Majesty, Your Royal Highnesses, Ladies and Gentlemen:

The Nobel Committee of the Norwegian Parliament (Storting) has awarded the Nobel Peace Prize for 1975 to Andrei Dmitrievich Sakharov.

In the will and testament that Alfred Nobel drew up prior to his death in 1896, he directed that the Peace Prize should be awarded to the person who had "done the most or the best work for fraternity between peoples, the abolition or reduction of standing armies, and for the holding and promotion of peace congresses".

As is only to be expected, the Nobel Committee's interpretation of these premises has varied in accordance with changing attitudes to the concept of peace over the years.

In the ranks of Peace Prize laureates during these last 74 years examples of this are readily available. The committee has rewarded: champions of the

---

1. *Time*, 13 November 2006.
2. Translated from Norwegian and published by Odelberg W. (ed), *Les Prix Nobel en 1975*, Stockholm, 1976. Copyright © The Nobel Foundation 1975.

ideas of international law; champions of social justice, such as Léon Jouhaux; for humanitarian achievements, such as Albert Schweitzer; for pacifist work, such as Bertha von Suttner and Carl von Ossietzky; for the promotion of human rights, such as René Cassin, Martin Luther King, and Albert Lutuli.

From the start the decisions made by the committee have frequently been the subject of criticism and debate. This need not, however, mean that they were incorrect. The Nobel Committee is an independent body, separate from any state authority, party, group, or individual. The basis of its decisions rests exclusively on the directions and intentions contained in Alfred Nobel's will and testament. For the committee to allow its work to be influenced in any way by fear or to be dictated by convenience or opportunism would constitute an unforgivable dereliction of its duties.

This year the Nobel Committee has awarded its Peace Prize to one of the great champions of human rights in our age. In setting forth its reasons for its present choice the committee states, inter alia*:*

"Sakharov's fearless personal commitment in upholding the fundamental principles for peace between men is a powerful inspiration for all true work for peace. Uncompromisingly and with unflagging strength Sakharov has fought against the abuse of power and all forms of violation of human dignity, and he has fought no less courageously for the idea of government based on the rule of law. In a convincing manner Sakharov has emphasised that man's inviolable rights provide thc only safe foundation for genuine and enduring international co-operation. In this way, in a particularly effective manner, working under difficult conditions, he has enhanced respect for the values that rally all true peace lovers."

We were repeatedly told during the great war that raged between 1940 and 1945 that this war was being fought in order to safeguard the human rights of future generations. Those who fought for this noble ideal, and the many millions who gave their lives to achieve it, won the war on the field of battle; but their great goal, the enduring establishment of human dignity, was not achieved.

During the post-war years the United Nations has worked energetically and untiringly to draw up and gain universal acceptance for a Universal Declaration and two Covenants on fundamental human rights. It has done so in the conviction that these rights and freedoms are absolute imperatives for the maintenance of lasting peace in the world. Most countries have accepted this idea.

And yet today – despite all the sacrifices and efforts that have been made – in every part of the world there are millions of people who do not enjoy the most elementary human rights; there are even regions where people who previously enjoyed these rights have forfeited them after the conclusion of the last war.

René Cassin, the architect of the Universal Declaration of Human Rights and the 1968 Peace Prize laureate, is fully aware of this. He has the following comment to make on the present situation:

"The Universal Declaration sets up an ideal for us to follow, and it lays down guidelines for our actions. Yet a glance at the world of today is sufficient to show that we still have a long way to go before we can achieve this ideal. Not a single country, even the most advanced, can pride itself on fulfilling all the articles of the declaration. We witness violations of the right to life. Murder and massacre are allowed to pass unpunished. Women are exploited, there is widespread famine, contempt for freedom of conscience and freedom of speech, widespread racial discrimination – all these evils are far too widespread to be overlooked."

Yet this tragic situation must not lead to resignation. On the contrary, it is a challenge to all responsible people, irrespective of national boundaries, to intensify their struggle to establish respect for human dignity and to rally around the courageous individuals who refuse to bow their necks to a yoke.

This year's prize winner, Andrei Sakharov, was born in Moscow in 1921. He studied physics at the University of Moscow, and attracted considerable attention at an early age with the publication of a number of scientific papers.

During the years from 1948 to 1968 Sakharov worked at a secret institute for nuclear research, as a member of a team of scientists engaged in the development of nuclear arms. Sakharov himself emphasises that his own contribution to the work of this team of scientists was not directed solely to military ends, but aimed as well at the harnessing of nuclear power for other purposes, for example, in industry and in the production of energy.

Although the Soviet Union in 1949, in common with the United States of America, had produced its own atom bomb, nevertheless the United States was far more advanced than the USSR in nuclear technology. Sakharov was of the opinion that, in the interests of peace, it was important to narrow this lead, in order to establish a balance in the arms race capable of deterring both parties from initiating a war.

At the exceptionally young age of 32, Sakharov was elected a member of the Russian Academy of Science. For his scientific work on behalf of his country he has twice been awarded the Order of Lenin, on one occasion the Stalin Prize, and on three separate occasions he has been honoured with the title of Hero of Socialist Labour.

In 1968, however, a significant change occurred in his status and way of life. He was removed from his research post and assigned work in the Physics Institute of the Academy of Science.

This change in Sakharov's circumstances and standing was a direct result of a change in his way of thinking. He describes this in his book Sakharov Speaks:

"Beginning in 1957 (not without the influence of statements on this subject made throughout the world by such people as Albert Schweitzer, Linus Pauling, and others) I felt myself responsible for the problem of radioactive contamination from nuclear explosions."

Sakharov made no secret of the fact that he had arrived at these conclusions; in fact, he expressed himself frankly to the authorities in letters, in which he set *forth his ideas on the situation. He hoped that this might provide a basis for a free and open exchange of opinion, but in this he was profoundly disappointed.*

In one important respect, however, Sakharov believes that his views have had some effect. This was when the USA and the Soviet Union completed an agreement in 1963 on a ban on nuclear tests in the atmosphere, in space, and in the ocean.

In 1968 Sakharov issued his famous essay Reflections on Progress, Peaceful Co-existence, and Intellectual Freedom. *Sakharov's* Reflections *are not based only on conditions in his own country; they are written from a global point of view and constitute an earnest appeal for peace addressed to responsible men and women in every country.*

The principal problem with which he deals in Reflections *is the threat of the total annihilation of our civilization which would result from a nuclear war. He maintains that this danger can only be averted by means of worldwide co-operation transcending national and ideological boundaries.*

In this connection he is particularly concerned with contacts between the USA and the Soviet Union. It is his belief that peaceful co-existence between these two super powers could be achieved if some measure of convergence were to take place between the political systems of these two states. Sakharov believes that this is the only alternative to a nuclear war which he describes as collective suicide.

As far as his own country's contribution to this convergence is concerned, he emphasises reforms such as democratisation, debureaucratisation, demilitarisation, and social and scientific progress. In close co-operation between these two super powers Sakharov also envisages the possibility for constructive joint approaches to the problems of world hunger, over-population, and pollution.

In his opinion, too, a substantial aid programme might provide a lasting foundation for a harmonious social and economic development of the Third World.

The contributions made by the industrial countries would, Sakharov believes, result in a considerable reduction in the amount of money spent by these countries on armaments.

As we all know, these are ideas that have been repeatedly debated in the United Nations. The philosophy at the back of this line of argument has, inter alia, found expression in the appeal which the United Nations made in 1970 asking rich member countries to allocate 1% of their gross national product for aid to the developing countries.

Sakharov's Reflections, which caused such a stir in large parts of the world, was the first publication in which he made a cohesive presentation of his views on the conditions necessary for a policy of détente and intellectual freedom. In subsequent publications, such as Sakharov Speaks and My Country and the World, his views on some of the problems he dealt with in Reflections have undergone a change. The reasons for this, he says, are the dramatic international developments of recent years, conversations he has had with people from his own country and abroad, as well as in his own wider personal experience. It is not so much the dream of the future with which he is preoccupied, as all the threatening dangers that may come between the dream and reality.

In assessing the ideas set forth in his Reflections Sakharov emphasises that at the time he wrote them, he was still living in an isolated and highly privileged scientific milieu. In an interview he stated:

"I was isolated from the people. Thus, in evaluating my essay of 1968 you must understand this and take into account the route I followed from work on thermonuclear weapons to my concern about the results of nuclear tests – the deaths of people, mutations, and other consequences. My life has been such that I began by confronting global problems and only later, more concrete, personal, and human ones."

It was Sakharov's contact with the daily life of fellow human beings and his concern that compelled him to commit himself to an intense struggle to find *a solution for problems which he described frankly in letters written to the authorities, and for which he demanded reforms.*

In an attempt to make his proposals known to a wider public, Sakharov became a founding member of the Moscow Human Rights Committee in 1970, together with friends and colleagues. The aim of the committee was to work, within the framework of the law, to institute constructive reforms for the promotion of human rights, in accordance with the humanist principles contained in the Declaration of Human Rights adopted by the United Nations in 1948.

Sakharov maintained that they should strive to achieve the abolition of secret trials; a new press law ensuring that people would have access to all available information; reform of the prison system; amnesty for political prisoners; the abolition of the death penalty; open frontiers; and a ban on the use of psychiatric institutes for political ends.

It must be gratifying for Sakharov to know that his ideas on the conditions necessary for peace and détente have found an echo in the Final Act of the Conference on Security and Cooperation in Europe, which was signed on 1 August this year by 35 states in Helsinki.

Section VII of the Final Act's Declaration of Principles states: "The participating States will respect human rights and fundamental freedoms, including the freedom of thought, conscience, religion or belief, for all without distinction as to race, sex, language or religion."

It goes on to state: "They will promote and encourage the effective exercise of civil, political, economic, social, cultural and other rights and freedoms all of which derive from the inherent dignity of the human person and are essential for his free and full development."

It is an historic event that the leading states of the world should have established in this document that human rights are an essential factor in détente between nations. No state and no politician can suppress or evade the moral and political obligations that these Articles impose by taking refuge in formalistic arguments couched in terms of international law. To do so would be a betrayal of mankind and of peace.

Andrei Dmitrievich Sakharov has shown that he is prepared to bear his share of the burden.

In the words of the Nobel Committee: "Andrei Sakharov's great contribution to peace is this, that he has fought in a particularly effective manner and under highly difficult conditions, in the greatest spirit of self-sacrifice, to obtain respect for these values that the Helsinki Final Act here declares to be its object."

Sakharov's struggle for human rights, for disarmament, and for co-operation between all nations has peace as its final goal. For his endeavours to improve the lot of people in every country we pay our tribute to him here today in awarding him the Nobel Peace Prize for 1975.

The Nobel Committee deeply deplores the fact that Andrei Sakharov has been prevented from being present here today in person to receive the Peace Prize. This is a fate he shares with the man who, 40 years ago in 1935, was awarded the Peace Prize. His name was Carl von Ossietzky.

The title page of Sakharov's celebrated Reflections of 1968 carries these words of Goethe as its epigraph:

> He alone is worthy of life and freedom
> Who each day does battle for them anew!

Andrei Dmitrievich Sakharov has in truth fulfilled Goethe's conditions for deserving both freedom and life.

I. Autobiography

In the preface to his *Memoirs*, published in 1990, Andrei Sakharov explains that he took up writing them because autobiographical narratives constitute an important part of mankind's memory. He also sought to set the record straight because much of what had been written about his life, his circumstances, and those close to him was grossly inaccurate.

> *I hope that my memoirs will appeal to a fairly large audience because of the extraordinary turns my life has taken: work at the munitions factory during the war, my career in theoretical physics, twenty years of developing thermonuclear weapons in a secret city ("the Installation"), research on controlled fusion, my statements on public issues, my activities in defence of human rights, the authorities' persecution of myself and my family, exile to Gorky, the years spent in isolation there, and my return to Moscow in the era of* perestroika.[3]

My fate was, in a way, an exceptional one ... Not from a false sense of modesty but from a desire to be accurate, I would say that my fate has proved to be greater than my personality. I only tried to reach the level of my destiny.[4]

An autobiographical note

Sakharov wrote this autobiographical note in March 1981 while in exile in Gorky.

I was born on 21 May 1921. My father was a teacher of physics and a well-known author of textbooks and books of popular science. My childhood was spent in a large communal apartment where most rooms were occupied by my family and relations and only a few by outsiders. Our home was imbued by the traditional spirit of a large close-knit family – respect for hard work and

---

3. Sakharov, A., *Memoirs*, Alfred A. Knopf, New York, 1990, p. xx.
4. Interview with Mark Levin during the 38th Conference of the Pugwash Movement, 29 August – 4 September 1988, first published in the newspaper *Molodezh Estonii* (Youth of Estonia), October 1988, and in English in Eisen J. (ed.), *The Glasnost Reader*, New American Library, 1990, pp. 328-41.

ability, mutual family support, love of literature and science. My father played the piano well, particularly Chopin, Grieg, Beethoven and Scriabin. During the years of the civil war, he earned a living by playing in a silent film theatre. I recall with particular fondness my grandmother, Maria Petrovna, who was the soul of the family. She died before the war at the age of 79. Family influences were especially strong in my case because my early schooling was at home, and I later had great difficulty relating to my class mates.

I finished school with distinction in 1938 and immediately enrolled at Moscow University's Physics Faculty. Here too I graduated with distinction in 1942, after we had been evacuated to Ashkhabad because of the war. In the summer and autumn of 1942 I lived for several weeks in Kovrov where I had first been sent to work after my graduation. Later I worked as a lumberjack in a remote rural settlement near Melekess. My first vivid impressions of the life of workers and peasants came from those difficult days. In September 1942, I was sent to a large munitions factory on the Volga where I worked as an engineer until 1945. At the factory I invented several devices to improve our quality control (in my university years I had not engaged in applied scientific work). In 1944, while still at the factory, I wrote several articles on theoretical physics which I sent to Moscow for review. These first works were never published, but they gave me self confidence, which is essential for every scientist.

In 1945 I became a doctoral student at the Lebedev Physics Institute of the USSR's Academy of Sciences. My supervisor, who influenced me enormously, was the great theoretical physicist, Igor Evgenievich Tamm, later a member of the Academy of Sciences and a Nobel Physics laureate. In 1948 I was included in a group of research scientists whose task was to develop a thermonuclear bomb. Tamm was the leader of this group. For the next twenty years I worked continuously under conditions of extraordinary tension and secrecy, first in Moscow and then in a special secret research centre [Arzamas-16 – 250 miles east of Moscow, and not far from Gorky]. We were all convinced of the vital significance of our work for achieving military equilibrium and were attracted by its grand scope.

In 1950 Igor Tamm and I undertook some of the earliest research on controlled thermonuclear reactions. We proposed principles for the magnetic confinement of hot plasma. I also proposed as an immediate technical objective the use of a thermonuclear reactor to produce fuel for atomic power plants. Research on controlled thermonuclear reactions is now receiving much attention throughout the world: the tokamak system which is closely related to our early ideas is under intensive study in many countries. Significant advances have now been made in this work. In 1952, I initiated experiments on the construction of magneto-implosive generators (devices which use chemical or nuclear explosions to produce ultra strong magnetic fields). In 1964 we attained a record magnetic field of 25 million gauss.

In 1953 I was elected member of the USSR Academy of Sciences. [This was part of Sakharov's reward for his major role in the development of the USSR's first thermonuclear weapon tested on 12 August 1953.]

From 1953 to 1968, my social and political views underwent a major evolution. In particular, my participation in the development of thermonuclear weapons between 1953 and 1962, and in the preparation and execution of thermonuclear tests, led to an increased awareness of the moral problems engendered by such activities. In the late 1950s I began a campaign to halt or to limit the testing of nuclear weapons. This brought me into conflict first with Nikita Khrushchev in 1961, and then with the Minister of Medium Machine Building, Efim Slavsky, in 1962. I helped to promote the 1963 Moscow Treaty banning nuclear weapon tests in the atmosphere, in outer space, and under water. From 1964, when I spoke out on problems of biology, and especially from 1967, I have been interested in an ever expanding circle of questions. In 1967 I joined the Committee for Lake Baikal.

My first appeals for victims of repression date from 1966-67. The time came in 1968 for a more detailed, public, and candid statement. Hence my essay Reflections on Progress, Peaceful Co-existence, and Intellectual Freedom. The same ideas were echoed seven years later in the title of my

Nobel lecture: "Peace, Progress, and Human Rights." I consider these themes of fundamental importance and closely interconnected. My 1968 essay was a turning point in my life. It quickly became widely known worldwide. The Soviet press was silent for a long time, and then began to refer to the essay very negatively. Many critics, even sympathetic ones, considered my ideas naive and impractical. Now, thirteen years later, it seems to me that these ideas foreshadowed important new directions in world and even Soviet politics.

From 1970 onwards the defence of human rights and the defence of victims of political repression became my first concern. My participation together with Chalidze and Tverdokhlebov, and later with Shafarevich and Podyapolsky in the Human Rights Committee was one expression of this position. (Grigory Podyapolsky's untimely death in March 1976 was a tragedy.) After my essay was published abroad in July 1968, I was removed from top secret work and "relieved" of my privileges in the Soviet establishment. The pressure on me and those close to me increased in 1972. As I learnt more about the spreading repressions, I felt obliged to speak out almost daily in defence of one victim or another. In those years I also often intervened on issues of peace and disarmament, on freedom of association, movement, information, and opinion, against capital punishment, on protection of the environment and on nuclear power plants.

In 1975 I was awarded the Nobel Peace Prize. This was a great honour for me, as well as a sign of respect for the entire human rights movement in the USSR. In January 1980 I was deprived of all my official Soviet awards (the Order of Lenin, three times Hero of Socialist Labour, the Lenin Prize, the State Prize) and banished to Gorky where I am virtually isolated and watched day and night by a policeman at my door. The regime's action lacks any legal basis. It is one more example of the intensified political repression in our country in recent years.

Since the summer of 1969 I have been a senior scientist at the Lebedev Physics Institute. My scientific interests are the theory of elementary particles, gravitation and cosmology.

I am not a professional politician. Perhaps that is why I am always bothered by questions concerning the usefulness and eventual results of my actions. I am inclined to believe that only moral criteria combined with unrestricted inquiry can provide a compass for these complex and contradictory problems. I shall refrain from specific predictions, but today, as always, I believe in the power of reason and the human spirit.

Andrei Sakharov
Gorky, 24 March 1981[5]

Arzamas 16 – "The Installation"

In 1950 our research group became part of a special institute. For the next 18 years I found myself caught up in the routine of a special world of military designers and inventors, special institutes, committees and learned councils, pilot plants and testing grounds. Every day I saw the huge material, intellectual and nervous resources of thousands of people being poured into the creation of a means of total destruction, something potentially capable of annihilating all human civilisation. I noticed that the control levers were in the hands of people who, though talented in their own way, were cynical. Until the summer of 1953 the chief of the atomic project was Beria, who ruled over millions of slave prisoners. Almost all the construction was done with their labour. Beginning in the late fifties, one got an increasingly clear picture of the collective might of the military-industrial complex and of its vigorous, unprincipled leaders, blind to everything except their "job". I was in a rather special position. As a theoretical scientist and inventor, relatively young and (moreover) not a party member, I was not involved in administrative responsibility and was exempt from party ideological discipline. My position enabled me to know and see a great deal. It compelled me to feel my own responsibility; and at the same time I could look upon this whole perverted system as an outsider. All this prompted me – especially in the ideological atmosphere that came into being after the death of Stalin and the Twentieth Congress of the CPSU – to reflect in general terms on the problems of peace and mankind and in particular on the problems of a thermonuclear war and its aftermath.[6]

---

5. Babyonyshev, A. (ed.), *On Sakharov*, trans. Daniels, G., Alfred A. Knopf, New York, 1982, pp. xi-xv.
6. Sakharov, A., *Sakharov Speaks*, Alfred A. Knopf, New York, 1974, pp. 31-2.

Sakharov did not mention his own family life in this autobiographical note, but he wrote about his marriage with Klavdia Vikhireva in his *Memoirs*:

> On November 19, 1942, the same day I began work at the laboratory of the Ulyanovsk cartridge factory, I met my wife-to-be, Klavdia Vikhireva – Klava.
>
> We had three children: our elder daughter, Tanya, born February 7, 1945; Lyuba, born July 28, 1949; and Dmitri, born August 14, 1957. Our children brought us a great deal of happiness; and, of course, like all children, problems, too. There were happy periods in our life that sometimes lasted for years, and I am grateful to Klava for them.[7]

Separated from his work and colleagues in 1968, dejected by the death of Klava in March 1969, his home disrupted by her death, Sakharov's life underwent major change. He returned to the theoretical department of the Lebedev Institute in 1969, joined the Human Rights Committee in 1970, and he found an ideal partner for his future life – Elena Bonner or "Lusia", Sakharov's pet name for his wife. They met through monitoring political trials in 1971 and attending the Thursday meetings of the Human Rights Committee. They married on 7 January 1972.

Exile in Gorky

On 8 January 1980, the Presidium of the Supreme Soviet adopted two decrees: "The Administrative Expulsion of Sakharov from Moscow" and "Revoking Sakharov's State Awards". For some years there had been discussions in the Politburo about possible means for disciplining Sakharov, but the decision to exile him to Gorky came almost immediately following Sakharov's call for the withdrawal of Soviet armed forces from Afghanistan, where they had been sent on 24 December 1979, and for a boycott of the 1980 Moscow Olympics if they failed to retreat. Sakharov, however, saw his banishment as part of a more general crackdown on dissent.

---

7. *Memoirs*, pp. 57-8.

Statement of 27 January 1980

On January 22, I was detained on the street and taken by force to the USSR Procurator's office. Alexander Rekunkov, First Deputy Procurator General of the USSR, informed me that I had been deprived of my title of Hero of Socialist Labour and of all decorations and prize awards, by decree of the Presidium of the Supreme Soviet of the USSR. I was asked to return the medals and orders and certificates, but I refused, believing that I was given them for good reason. Rekunkov also informed me of the decision to banish me to the city of Gorky, which is closed to foreigners.

On the same day, with my wife, Elena Bonner, who was allowed to go with me, I was taken by special flight to Gorky, where the city's deputy procurator explained the conditions of the regime decreed for me – overt surveillance, prohibitions against going beyond the city limits, against meeting with foreigners and "criminal elements", and against correspondence and telephone conversations with foreigners, including scientific and purely personal contacts, even with my children and grandchildren. I was instructed to report three times a week to the police station, and threatened that I would be taken there by force if I refused to obey.

The authorities are completely isolating me from the outside world. The house is surrounded 24 hours a day by police and the KGB, who keep away all visitors, including our friends. Telephone connections with Moscow and Leningrad are cut off... These restrictions also apply to my wife, who is supposedly "free".

Even in prison, there is more possibility of communication with the outside world.

No longer youngsters and not in the best of health, we are completely deprived of help from our friends and of medical care from our doctors.

These repressive actions were taken against me at a time of a deteriorating international situation and intensified persecution of dissidents within the country.

The actions of the authorities against me are aimed at making the continuation of my public activities completely impossible. They are aimed at humiliating and discrediting me and at the same time making possible further repressive measures against all dissident groups in the country (with less possibility of the world finding out about them), and also further international adventures. ...

Soviet representatives are trying to calm world opinion by saying that I will be able to continue scientific work and that there is no threat of criminal prosecution against me. But I am prepared to stand public and open trial. I do not need a gilded cage. I need the right to fulfil my public duty as my conscience dictates.[8]

This is how Sakharov described his life in Gorky one and a half years later.

I live in an apartment with a policeman stationed at the door round-the-clock. I often live completely alone, since my wife is forced to spend a great deal of time in Moscow.

I spend most of my time at my desk, reading and writing. In order to listen to Voice of America and other Western radio stations I have to go far from my house to escape my own personal jamming system, but the regular jamming is sufficiently strong that often I still can't hear anything. Household chores take up some of my time – I often straighten up the apartment before my wife's arrival, I go to buy bread, and I take my wash to the laundry. I do all these things quite slowly. I rarely take walks when my wife is away, but when she is here, we go for walks, sometimes we go to movies. Three times in the past year and a half we attended concerts.

I wish to devote the major part of my energy to scientific work. I'm especially interested in elementary particle physics and cosmology. But it is simply

---

8. This open statement was first published in the *New York Times*, 29 January 1980.

impossible to talk of "quiet scientific work" when I am kept isolated in illegal exile and the repeated thefts of my scientific and other manuscripts require me to spend enormous energy simply restoring those works.[9]

On 22 November 1981, having exhausted all other means, Sakharov and Elena Bonner began a joint hunger strike for Liza, their daughter-in-law, to join their son Alexei who had emigrated to the United States in 1978, at Sakharov's urging. Authorisation for her to leave was received on 7 December and the Sakharovs ended their hunger strike the next day. On 15 December, Sakharov wrote the following note:

We are deeply grateful to everyone who supported us in these bad times – to the statesmen, the religious leaders and public personalities, to the scientists and journalists, to our dear ones and friends, to those whom we know and to those we do not know.

It was a struggle not only for the life and happiness of our children, not only for my honour and dignity, but also for the right of every human being to be free and happy, for the right to live in accordance with one's ideas and beliefs, and in the final count – for all prisoners of conscience.

Wishing Liza a happy journey, I hope for the reunion of all who are separated, and I recall the wonderful words of Mihajlo Mihajlov: "Motherland is neither a geographical nor a national concept – motherland is freedom."[10]

On 2 May 1984, Elena Bonner was detained and searched at Gorky airport. She was placed under investigation, and charged with slandering the Soviet system. She was convicted on 10 August 1984, and sentenced to five years' internal exile to be served in Gorky. This brought to an end her visits to Moscow and the Sakharovs' main means of contact with the outside world.

---

9. *A Chronicle of Human Rights in the USSR*, No. 43, Khronika Press, New York, pp. 17-18.
10. *A Chronicle of Human Rights in the USSR*, No. 44, pp. 10-11.

Increasingly anxious about his wife's health and determined to secure permission for her to travel to the USA for the medical treatment she so badly needed, Sakharov began a series of debilitating hunger strikes in May 1984, which he continued until October 1985. The following month, Elena Bonner left Gorky for Boston where she was reunited with her relatives. On 14 January 1986, she had open heart surgery with six bypasses to repair her heart. She returned to Gorky at the beginning of June.

Return to Moscow

Andrei Sakharov's exile was ended by Mikhail Gorbachev, who had succeeded Konstantin Chernenko as General Secretary of the Communist Party in 1985. On 9 December 1986, the party's Central Committee annulled the decree banishing Sakharov and pardoned Elena Bonner and on 16 December, Gorbachev made a personal phone call to Sakharov, inviting him to return to Moscow.

Sakharov writes about the tumultuous years that followed in his book *Moscow and Beyond*, a continuation of his *Memoirs*.

On the morning of December 23, 1986, Lusia and I stepped off the train at Moscow's Yaroslavl Station onto a platform teeming with reporters from all over the world – and, as I learned later, from the Soviet Union as well. It took me forty minutes to make my way through the crowd. Lusia had been separated from me, hundreds of flashbulbs blinded me, and microphones were continually thrust into my face while I tried to respond to the barrage of questions. This impromptu media event was the prototype of many to follow: the whole scene offered a preview of the hurly-burly life that now awaited us.

I spoke of prisoners of conscience, naming many; of the need to pull Soviet troops out of Afghanistan; of my thoughts on the Strategic Defence Initiative (SDI) and Soviet insistence that American renunciation of SDI was a precondition for negotiations on nuclear weapons – the so-called "package principle"; of perestroika *and* glasnost *and of the contradictory and complex nature of these processes. For a while, I gave several interviews a day to newspapers, magazines, and television companies from all over the world, but fortunately the pace slackened a bit after January. ...*

Lusia and I were almost buried under the load of those first few months; but we had no choice, we had to carry on. What has life in Moscow been like since our return? I have to spend time preparing written responses (which Lusia types out) for almost all major interviews; I just can't do it any other way. ...

Once the mass release of political prisoners began, Lusia kept a running list in order to report to the news agencies their names and any hitches that developed. The foreign correspondents (and the radio commentators) often made egregious errors, so that instead of Lusia's report on a hunger strike by the Ukrainian dissident Mykola Rudenko, who was demanding information on the fate of his confiscated archive, we would hear Western broadcasters saying that Academician Sakharov had announced a hunger strike by Rudenko demanding permission to emigrate, and that Sakharov's wife had asserted that this affair demonstrated the negative side of Kremlin policy – words she never could or would have said, since they're not her style, to put it mildly. There were comparable mistakes almost every day; even my statements on SDI came out garbled.

That was our everyday life. Perhaps I have delusions of grandeur, but I want to believe that this wasn't all wasted motion or a game. I don't mind if the process was inefficient so long as it actually promoted the release of political prisoners, the preservation of peace, and disarmament.

What did I say in my first interviews? I stressed over and over again that the release of all prisoners of conscience would demonstrate the depth, authenticity, and irreversibility of democratic change in our country, that the continuing detention of people who had spoken out too soon for glasnost *betrayed a lack of consistency in the current course. I would then name up to a dozen prisoners whose cases I knew well.*[11]

* * *

---

11. Sakharov, A., *Moscow and Beyond*, Alfred A. Knopf, New York, 1990, pp. 3-5.

What other thoughts did I have a year after my return to Moscow? What hopes for the future?

I dreamed of science. Perhaps I would never accomplish anything of importance. I'd lost too many years, first in work on weapons, then in public activity and finally in exile in Gorky. Science demands utter concentration, and all these things were distractions. And yet, just being here to see the great advances in high-energy physics and in cosmology is an exhilarating experience that makes life worth living – and of course, there are all sorts of other things in the world that everyone can enjoy.

I expected to maintain at least a nominal interest in some of the undertakings where my name could make a difference: controlled thermonuclear fusion; the underground siting of nuclear reactors; and the use of underground nuclear explosions to control earthquakes.

I realized that Lusia and I would not be able to escape from our civic concerns, even after all the prisoners of conscience were released and large-scale emigration was permitted. We would have to adapt to the challenges that were bound to come while at the same time preserving our integrity. ...[12]

The last three years of Sakharov's life are summarised in the foreword to the English version of the *Memoirs*: "Back from Gorky, Sakharov moved to fulfil – sometimes reluctantly, sometimes awkwardly, but always with courage and integrity, discernment and compassion – his responsibilities as spokesman for the liberal intelligentsia." He was elected to the presidium of the Academy of Sciences, chosen as one of five directors of the Inter-regional Group of People's Deputies, appointed a member of the governmental commission to draft a new Soviet constitution, and made a member of the Governing Council of "Memorial", the society founded to preserve the memory of Stalin's victims. He served as an unofficial national ombudsman "travelling round the Soviet

---

12. Ibid., pp. 35-37.

Union to lend his support to persons suffering from official abuse. And at the June 1989 Congress of People's Deputies, with his fervent pleas for a radical reformation of the Soviet system and an end to the Communist Party's privileged position, he attempted to reinvigorate *perestroika* and to mend the uneasy collaboration between state and society inaugurated by Gorbachev's phone call. Only a few days before his death, he completed the preliminary draft of a new constitution for the 'Union of Soviet Republics of Europe and Asia' and began circulating it among his associates for comment."[13]

In his Epilogue to *Moscow and Beyond*, which he completed in September 1989, Sakharov wrote:

Of course, completing a book gives one a sense of crossing a frontier, of finality. As Pushkin put it, "Why is this strange sadness troubling me?" At the same time, there is an awareness of the powerful flow of life, which began before us and will continue after.

There is the miracle of science. I don't believe that we will come up with a theory that will explain everything in the universe anytime soon (and perhaps never), but I have seen fantastic advances just in the course of my own lifetime, and there is no reason to expect the stream to dry up: on the contrary, I believe it will broaden and branch out. ...

A few words about my own family, children, and grandchildren. There is much I have failed to do, sometimes because of my natural disposition to procrastinate, sometimes because of sheer physical impossibility, sometimes because of the resistance of my daughters and son which I could not overcome. But I have never stopped thinking about this.

And finally, Lusia, my wife. Truly, she is the only person who shares my thoughts and feelings. Lusia prompts me to understand much that I would

---

13. *Memoirs*, p. xvi.

otherwise miss because of my restrained personality, and to act accordingly. She is a great organizer, and serves as my brain centre. We are together. This gives life meaning.[14]

Sakharov died of a heart attack at home in Moscow on 14 December 1989 at the age of 68. He is buried in Moscow's Vostryakovskoye Cemetery.

---

14. *Moscow and Beyond*, pp. 159-60.

II. Andrei Sakharov's vision and world view

Prologue to *My Country and the World*

Sakharov was 24 years old when the Second World War ended. In the Prologue to his book, *My Country and the World*, published in 1975, Sakharov writes:

The contours of the most serious and urgent problems facing the world today began to emerge and first became apparent to me and many others of my generation in the years following World War II.

Thirty years ago a bloody and most destructive war had just come to an end, leaving in its wake a sea of human misery on so vast a scale that its traces still persist. Famine raged over extensive regions of the planet, claiming millions of lives and threatening to spread further. Science and technology were laying the foundations for the "green revolution" which was supposed to curb that dreaded calamity. But scientific progress was also bringing nearer another danger for mankind – ecological catastrophe. Only a few individuals then realised the magnitude of this new peril.

The H-bomb did not exist. But the atomic bomb had already cast its shadows over the world, and for the first time mankind was facing the possibility of total annihilation. In Hiroshima and Nagasaki radiation victims were dying every day.

The fires of civil war had broken out in China, Stalinism had taken hold of the socialist countries and the bodies and souls of millions were being crushed in its terrible grasp. The furnaces of Auschwitz had gone out. But thousands were perishing daily in the frozen mines of Kolyma, Norilsk, and Vorkuta and in Stalin's "death brigades". The number of Gulag victims had already reached the enormous toll of 20 million.

In those years, public-spirited and penetrating thinkers – physicists and mathematicians, economists, jurists, public figures, and philosophers – advanced ideas occasioned by their profound anxiety for the fate of mankind. They included Einstein, Russell, Bohr, Cassin, and many others who anticipated the problems of our day, even though they did not understand many things concealed from the West by the Iron Curtain.

They called for the defence of human rights throughout the world, for national altruism, for the realisation of an open world. (In explaining this concept, Niels Bohr emphasised that nothing should inhibit the exchange of information or freedom of movement.) They called for demilitarisation, for aid to underdeveloped countries, for strengthening the UN, for world government.

Even at that time I managed to find out about Bohr's statement. But it was only twenty years later, at the height of the 1968 "Prague Spring," that after many years of experience of associating with remarkable individuals, of meditation, I decided to publish an essay whose basic thrust was inspired by those ideas. The essay, later published as a book, was called Reflections on Progress, Peaceful Co-existence and Freedom. It was widely read, especially in the West, as one of the first statements of its kind from the mute inner recesses of the socialist countries. And to this day I have not basically changed the views I formulated at that time.[15]

Conclusion of Niels Bohr's open letter to the United Nations

Within any community it is only possible for its citizens to strive together for common welfare on a basis of public knowledge of the general conditions in the country. Likewise, real co-operation between nations on problems of common concern presupposes free access to all information of importance for their relations. Any argument for upholding barriers for information and intercourse, based on concern for national ideals or interests, must be weighed against the beneficial effects of common enlightenment and the relieved tension resulting from openness.

In the search for a harmonious relationship between the life of the individual and the organization of the community, there have always been and will ever remain

---

15. Prologue to *My Country and the World*, Alfred A. Knopf, New York, 1975, pp. 3-5.

many problems to ponder and principles for which to strive. However, to make it possible for nations to benefit from the experience of others and to avoid mutual misunderstanding of intentions, free access to information and unhampered opportunity for exchange of ideas must be granted everywhere. ...

The development of technology has now reached a stage where the facilities for communication have provided the means for making all mankind a co-operating unit, and where at the same time fatal consequences to civilization may ensue unless international divergences are considered as issues to be settled by consultation based on free access to all relevant information.

The very fact that knowledge is in itself the basis for civilization points directly to openness as the way to overcome the present crisis. Whatever judicial and administrative international authorities may eventually have to be created in order to stabilize world affairs, it must be realized that full mutual openness, only, can effectively promote confidence and guarantee common security. ...

I turn to the United Nations with these considerations in the hope that they may contribute to the search for a realistic approach to the grave and urgent problems confronting humanity. The arguments presented suggest that every initiative from any side towards the removal of obstacles for free mutual information and intercourse would be of the greatest importance in breaking the present deadlock and encouraging others to take steps in the same direction. The efforts of all supporters of international co-operation, individuals as well as nations, will be needed to create in all countries an opinion to voice, with ever increasing clarity and strength, the demand for an open world.

Copenhagen, 9 June 1950 [16]

Reflections on Progress, Co-existence and Intellectual Freedom

Sakharov's essay *Reflections on Progress, Co-existence and Intellectual Freedom* appeared at the end of April 1968 and was widely circulated in *samizdat* [self-publishing]. It was then published abroad, first in the Dutch

---

16. Published in Copenhagen by Schultz Forlag J. H. Reprinted in the *Bulletin of the Atomic Scientists*, Volume 6, Number 7 (June 1950) at: www.atomicarchive.com/Docs/Deterrence/BohrUN.shtml.

newspaper *Het Parool* on 6 July, and then in full in the *New York Times* on 22 July.[17] Sakharov lost his security clearance that summer, and was dismissed from his position as deputy director of scientific research at Arzamas-16. A year later, he was offered work as a senior scientist in the Department of Theoretical Physics of the Lebedev Physics Institute.

Sakharov writes in his *Memoirs* that the title he gave to his essay "seemed appropriate in tone for a non-specialist inviting his readers to join him in a discussion of public issues." As he explained:

> *I wanted to alert my readers to the grave perils threatening the human race – thermonuclear extinction, ecological catastrophe, famine, an uncontrolled population explosion, alienation, and dogmatic distortion of our conception of reality. I argued for convergence, for a rapprochement of the socialist and capitalist systems that could eliminate or substantially reduce these dangers, which had been increased several times over by the division of the world into opposing camps. Economic, social, and ideological convergence should bring about a scientifically governed, democratic, pluralist society free of intolerance and dogmatism, a humane society which would care for the Earth and its future, and would embody the positive features of both systems.*[18]

Sakharov began *Reflections* with two theses that he believed were shared by very many people throughout the world. These concerned the destruction threatened by the division of mankind and the need for intellectual freedom. He divided the essay into "Dangers" and the "The Basis of Hope", and ended with a "Summary of Proposals". Recognising that much of what he had written was controversial, he invited discussion and debate.

Sakharov's theses

1. The division of mankind threatens it with destruction. Civilization is imperilled by: a universal thermonuclear war, catastrophic hunger for most of mankind,

---

17. Sakharov states in his *Memoirs* that the International Publishers Association released statistics showing that during 1968 and 1969 more than 18 million copies of the essay were published around the world. *Memoirs*, p. 288.
18. Ibid., p. 282.

stupefaction from the narcotic of "mass culture", and bureaucratized dogmatism, a spreading of mass myths that put entire peoples and continents under the power of cruel and treacherous demagogues and destruction or degeneration from the unforeseeable consequences of swift changes in the conditions of life on our planet.

In the face of these perils, any action increasing the division of mankind, any preaching of the incompatibility of world ideologies and nations is madness and a crime. Only universal co-operation under conditions of intellectual freedom and the lofty moral ideals of socialism and labour, accompanied by the elimination of dogmatism and pressures of the concealed interests of ruling classes, will preserve civilization.

The reader will understand that ideological collaboration cannot apply to those fanatical, sectarian and extremist ideologies that reject all possibility of rapprochement, discussion, and compromise, for example, the ideologies of fascist, racist, militaristic, and Maoist demagogy.

Millions of people throughout the world are striving to put an end to poverty. They despise oppression, dogmatism, and demagogy (and their more extreme manifestations – racism, fascism, Stalinism and Maoism). They believe in progress based on the use, under conditions of social justice and intellectual freedom, of all the positive experience accumulated by mankind.

2. The second basic thesis is that intellectual freedom is essential to human society – freedom to receive and impart information, freedom for open-minded and unfearing debate, and freedom from pressure by officialdom and prejudices. Such a trinity of freedom of thought is the only guarantee against an infection of people by mass myths, which, in the hands of treacherous hypocrites and demagogues, can be transformed into bloody dictatorship. Freedom of thought is the only guarantee of the feasibility of a scientific democratic approach to politics, economy, and culture.

But freedom of thought is under a triple threat in modern society – from the deliberate opium of mass culture, from cowardly, egotistic and philistine ideologies, and from the ossified dogmatism of a bureaucratic oligarchy and its favourite weapon, ideological censorship. Therefore, freedom of thought requires the defence of all thinking and honest people. This is a mission not only for the intelligentsia, but for all strata of society, particularly its most active and organized stratum, the working class. The worldwide dangers of war, famine, cults of personality, and bureaucracy – these are perils for all of mankind.

Recognition by the working class and the intelligentsia of their common interests has been a striking phenomenon of the present day. The most progressive, internationalist and dedicated element of the intelligentsia is, in essence, part of the working class, and the most advanced, educated, internationalist and broad-minded part of the working class is part of the intelligentsia.

This position of the intelligentsia in society renders senseless any loud demands that the intelligentsia subordinate its strivings to the will and interests of the working class (in the Soviet Union, Poland and other socialist countries). What these demands really mean is subordination to the will of the Party or, even more specifically, to the Party's central apparatus and its officials. Who will guarantee that these officials always express the genuine interests of the working class as a whole and the genuine interests of progress rather than their own caste interests?

Dangers

Under "Dangers", Sakharov reflected on the threat of nuclear war; Vietnam and the Middle East; international tensions; hunger and overpopulation; racism; pollution of the environment; police dictatorships and the threat to intellectual freedom. His reflections on pollution and on dictatorships follow.

Pollution of the environment

We live in a swiftly changing world. Industrial and water-engineering projects, cutting down forests, ploughing up virgin lands, the use of poisonous chemicals – all such activity is changing the face of the earth, our "habitat".

Scientific study of all the inter-relationships in nature and the consequences of our interference clearly lag behind the changes. Large amounts of harmful wastes of industry and transport are being dumped into the air and water, including cancer-inducing substances. Will the safe limit be passed everywhere, as has already happened in a number of places?

Carbon dioxide from the burning of coal is altering the heat-reflecting qualities of the atmosphere. Sooner or later, this will reach a dangerous level. But we do not know when. Poisonous chemicals used in agriculture are penetrating the body of man and animal directly, and in more dangerous compounds are causing serious damage to the brain, the nervous system, blood-forming organs, the liver and other organs. Here, too, the safe limit can be easily crossed, but the question has not been fully studied and it is difficult to control all these processes.

The use of antibiotics in poultry raising has led to the development of new disease-causing microbes that are resistant to antibiotics.

I could also mention the problems of dumping detergents and radioactive wastes, erosion and salinization of soils, the flooding of meadows, the cutting of forests on mountain slopes and in watersheds, the destruction of birds and other useful wildlife like toads and frogs, and many other examples of senseless despoliation caused by local, temporary, bureaucratic and egotistical interest and sometimes simply by questions of bureaucratic prestige, as in the sad fate of Lake Baikal.

The problem of geohygiene is highly complex and closely tied to economic and social problems. This problem can therefore not be solved on a national and especially not on a local basis. The salvation of our environment requires that we overcome our divisions and the pressure of temporary, local interests. Otherwise, the Soviet Union will poison the United States with its wastes and vice versa. At present, this is a hyperbole. But with a 10 percent annual increase of wastes, the increase over a hundred years will be multiplied twenty thousand times.

Dictatorships

An extreme reflection of the dangers confronting modern social development is the growth of racism, nationalism and militarism and, in particular, the rise of demagogic, hypocritical, and monstrously cruel dictatorial police regimes. Foremost are the regimes of Stalin, Hitler and Mao Tse-tung and a number of extremely reactionary regimes in smaller countries, such as Spain, Portugal, South Africa, Greece, Albania, Haiti and other Latin American countries.

These tragic developments have always derived from the struggle of selfish individual and group interests, the struggle for unlimited power, suppression of intellectual freedom, the spread of intellectually simplified, narrow-minded mass myths (the myth of race, of land and blood, the myth about the Jewish danger, anti-intellectualism, the concept of lebensraum *in Germany, the myth about the sharpening of the class struggle and proletarian infallibility bolstered by the cult of Stalin and by exaggeration of the contradictions with capitalism in the Soviet Union, the myth about Mao Tse-tung, extreme Chinese nationalism and its resurrection of the lebensraum concept, of anti-intellectualism, extreme anti-humanism and certain prejudices of peasant socialism in China).*

The world will never forget the burning of books in the squares of German cities, the hysterical, cannibalistic speeches of the fascist "fuehrers" and their even more cannibalistic plans for the destruction of entire peoples, including the Russians. Fascism began a partial realization of these plans during the war it unleashed, annihilating prisoners of war and hostages, burning villages, carrying out a criminal policy of genocide (during the war, the main blow of genocide was aimed at the Jews, a policy that apparently was also meant to be provocative, especially in the Ukraine and Poland).

We shall never forget the kilometre-long trenches filled with bodies, the gas chambers, the SS dogs, the fanatical doctors, the piles of women's hair, suitcases with gold teeth, and fertilizer from the factories of death.

Analyzing the causes of Hitler's coming to power, we will never forget the role of German and international monopolist capital. We also will not forget the criminally sectarian and dogmatically narrow policies of Stalin and his associates, setting Socialists and Communists against one another.

Fascism lasted twelve years in Germany. Stalinism lasted twice as long in the Soviet Union. There are many common features but also certain differences. Stalinism exhibited a much more subtle kind of hypocrisy and demagogy, with reliance not on an openly cannibalistic program like Hitler's but on a progressive, scientific, and popular socialist ideology.

This served as a convenient screen for deceiving the working class, for weakening the vigilance of the intellectuals and other rivals in the struggle for power, with the treacherous and sudden use of the machinery of torture, execution and informants, intimidating and making fools of millions of people, the majority of whom were neither cowards nor fools. As a consequence of this "specific feature" of Stalinism, it was the Soviet people, its most active, talented, and honest representatives, who suffered the most terrible blow.

At least ten to fifteen million people perished in the torture chambers of the NKVD from torture and execution, in camps for exiled kulaks *[rich peasants] and so-called semi-*kulaks *and members of their families and in camps "without the right of correspondence" (which were in fact the prototypes of the fascist death camps, where, for example, thousands of prisoners were machine-gunned because of "overcrowding" or as a result of "special orders").*

People perished in the mines of Norilsk and Vorkuta from freezing, starvation and exhausting labour, at countless construction projects, in timber-cutting, building of canals, or simply during transportation in prison trains, in the overcrowded holds of "death ships" in the Sea of Okhotsk, and during the resettlement of entire peoples, the Crimean Tatars, the Volga Germans, the Kalmyks, and peoples of the Caucasus region. Readers of the literary journal Novy Mir *recently could read for themselves a description of the "road of death" between Norilsk and Igarka [in northern Siberia].*

Stalinist dogmatism and isolation from real life was demonstrated particularly in the countryside, in the policy of unlimited exploitation and the predatory forced deliveries at "symbolic" prices, in almost serf-like enslavement of the peasantry, the depriving of peasants of the simplest means of mechanization, and the appointment of collective farm chairmen on the basis of their cunning and obsequiousness. The results are evident – a profound and hard-to-correct destruction of the economy and way of life in the countryside, which, by "the law of interconnected vessels", damaged industry as well.

The inhuman character of Stalinism was demonstrated by the repression of prisoners of war who survived fascist camps and then were thrown into Stalinist camps, the anti-worker "decrees", the criminal exile of entire peoples condemned to slow death, the unenlightened, zoological anti-Semitism that was characteristic of Stalin bureaucracy, and the NKVD (and Stalin personally), the Ukrainophobia characteristic of Stalin, and the draconian laws for the protection of socialist property (five years' imprisonment for stealing grain from the fields and so forth) that served mainly as a means of fulfilling the demands of the "slave market".

Our country has started on the path of cleansing away the foulness of Stalinism. "We are squeezing the slave out of ourselves drop by drop" (an expression of Anton Chekhov). We are learning to express our opinions, without taking the lead from the bosses and without fearing for our lives.

The beginning of this arduous and far from straight path evidently dates from the report of Nikita Khrushchev to the Twentieth Congress of the Soviet Communist Party. This bold speech, which came as a surprise to Stalin's accomplices in crime, and a number of associated measures – the release of hundreds of thousands of political prisoners and their rehabilitation, steps toward a revival of the principles of peaceful coexistence and toward a revival of democracy – oblige us to value highly the historic role of Khrushchev despite his wilful and regrettable mistakes in subsequent years and despite the fact that Khrushchev, while Stalin was alive, was one of his collaborators in crime, occupying a number of influential posts.

The exposure of Stalinism in our country still has a long way to go. It is imperative, of course, that we publish all authentic documents, including the archives of the NKVD, and conduct nationwide investigations. It would be highly useful for the international authority of the Soviet Communist Party and the ideals of socialism if, as was planned in 1964 but never carried out, the party were to announce the "symbolic" expulsion of Stalin, murderer of millions of Party members, and at the same time the political rehabilitation of the victims of Stalinism.

From 1936 to 1939 more than 1.2 million Party members, half of the total membership, were arrested. Only fifty thousand regained freedom; the others were tortured during interrogation or were shot (six hundred thousand) or died in camps. Only in isolated cases were the rehabilitated allowed to assume responsible posts; even fewer were permitted to take part in the investigation of crimes of which they had been witnesses or victims.

We are often told lately not to "rub salt into wounds". This is usually being said by people who suffered no wounds. Actually only the most meticulous analysis of the past and of its consequences will now enable us to wash off the blood and dirt that befouled our banner.

Summary of proposals

In conclusion, I will sum up a number of the concrete proposals of varying degrees of importance that have been discussed in the text. These proposals, addressed to the leadership of the country, do not exhaust the content of the article.

The strategy of peaceful co-existence and collaboration must be deepened in every way. Scientific methods and principles of international policy will have to be worked out, based on scientific prediction of the immediate and more distant consequences.

The initiative must be seized in working out a broad program of struggle against hunger.

A law on press and information must be drafted, widely discussed and adopted, with the aim not only of ending irresponsible and irrational censorship, but also of encouraging self study in our society, fearless discussion, and the search for truth. The law must provide for the material resources of freedom of thought.

All anti-constitutional laws and decrees violating human rights must be abrogated.

Political prisoners must be amnestied and some of the recent political trials must be reviewed (for example, the Daniel-Sinyavsky and Ginzburg-Galanskov cases).[19] The camp regime of political prisoners must be promptly relaxed.

The exposure of Stalin must be carried through to the end, to the complete truth, and not just to the carefully weighed half truth dictated by caste considerations. The influence of neo-Stalinists in our political life must be restricted in every way.

Economic reform must be deepened in every way and the area of experimentation expanded, with conclusions based on results.

A law on geohygiene must be adopted after broad discussion, and ultimately become part of world efforts in this field.[20]

---

19. The writers Yuli Daniel and Andrei Sinyavsky were arrested in 1965, and convicted in February 1966 of anti-Soviet propaganda for sending abroad literary works that the authorities contended were slanderous to the state. Daniel was sentenced to five years in labour camp and Sinyavsky to seven. Aleksandr Ginzburg, a poet, and Yury Galanskov, a poet and editor, were convicted in January 1968 on charges growing out of their protest of the Daniel-Sinyavsky case, and sentenced to five and seven years' imprisonment respectively. Galanskov died in a prison camp in 1972.
20. The *New York Times*, 22 July 1968. The essay can be found on the website of the Andrei Sakharov Museum and Public Centre at: www.sakharov-center.ru/asfconf2009/english/node/20.

In March 1970, together with the physicist Valentin Turchin and historian Roy Medvedev, Sakharov sent a letter to the leadership of the Soviet Union (Brezhnev, Kosygin and Podgorny) calling for the introduction of democracy and intellectual freedom as essential for the advancement of science and performance of the economy.[21] On 5 March 1971, Sakharov sent a Memorandum to General Secretary Brezhnev, requesting a discussion of "urgent problems and questions", also partially raised in his 1968 *Reflections* and 1970 letter.[22] He informed Brezhnev that he, together with Valery Chalidze and Andrei Tverdokhlebov, had created a "Human Rights Committee" to study the problem of safeguarding human rights and to promote the growth of legal awareness, and that the Committee sought a dialogue with the country's leadership and a frank and public discussion of problems of human rights. Sakharov allowed a year for a considered reply, which did not come. In June 1972, he added a postscript and gave it and the Memorandum to foreign correspondents and to *samizdat*.

Postscript to Memorandum

I began my activity approximately ten to twelve years ago, when I realized the criminal character of a possible thermonuclear war and of thermonuclear tests in the atmosphere. Since then I have revised my views to a considerable extent, particularly since the year 1968, which began for me with my writing Reflections on Progress, Coexistence, and Intellectual Freedom, *and ended, as for everybody else, with the rumbling of tanks in the streets of unyielding Prague.*

As before, I cannot fail to appreciate the great and beneficial changes (social, cultural and economic) that have taken place in our country in the last fifty years, realizing, however, that analogous changes have taken place in many countries and that they are a manifestation of worldwide progress.

---

21. *Sakharov Speaks*, pp. 116-34. Sakharov was the principal author of this letter.
22. Ibid., pp. 136-50.

As before, I consider that it will be possible to overcome the tragic conflicts and dangers of our time only through the convergence of capitalism and the socialist regime.

In capitalist countries this process must be accompanied by further improvement in the protection of workers' rights and a reduction in the role of militarism and its influence on political life. In socialist countries it is also essential to reduce the militarization of the economy and the role of a messianic ideology. It is vitally necessary to weaken the extreme forms of centralism and Party-state bureaucratic monopoly, both in the economic sphere of production and consumption, and in the sphere of ideology and culture.

As before, I consider the democratization of society, the development of openness in public affairs, the rule of law, and the safeguarding of basic human rights to be of decisive importance.

As before, I hope that society will evolve along these lines under the influence of technological-economic progress, although my prognoses have become more cautious.

It seems to me now, more than ever before, that the only true guarantee for safeguarding human values in the chaos of uncontrollable changes and tragic upheavals is man's freedom of conscience and his moral yearning for the good.

Our society is infected by apathy, hypocrisy, petit bourgeois egoism, and hidden cruelty. The majority of representatives of its upper stratum – the Party apparatus, the government and the highest, most successful layers of the intelligentsia – cling tenaciously to their open and secret privileges and are profoundly indifferent to the infringement of human rights, the interests of progress, security and the future of mankind. Others, though deeply concerned in their hearts, cannot allow themselves any freedom of thought and are condemned to the torture of internal conflict. Drunkenness has assumed the dimensions of a national calamity. It is one of the symptoms of *the moral degradation of a society that is sinking ever deeper into a state of chronic alcoholic poisoning.*

The country's spiritual regeneration demands the elimination of those conditions that drive people into becoming hypocritical and time-serving, and that lead to feelings of impotence, discontent and disillusionment. Everybody must be assured, in deed and not just in word, of equal opportunities for advancement in his work, in education and cultural growth; and the system of privileges in all spheres of consumption must be abolished. Full intellectual freedom must be assured and all forms of persecution of beliefs must cease. A radical educational reform is essential. These ideas are the basis of many proposals in the memorandum.

In particular, the memorandum mentions the problem of improvement in the material condition and independence of two of the most numerous and socially significant groups of the intelligentsia, the teachers and medical workers. The sorry state of popular education and of the health service is carefully hidden from the eyes of foreigners, but cannot remain secret from those who wish to see. A free health service and education are no more than an economic illusion in a society in which all surplus value is expropriated and distributed by the state. The hierarchical class structure of our society, with its system of privileges, is reflected in a particularly pernicious way in the health service and education. The condition of the health service and of popular education is clearly revealed in the rundown state of public hospitals, in the poverty of the village schools, with their overcrowded classes, the poverty and low standing of the teacher, and the official hypocrisy in teaching, which inculcates in the rising generation a spirit of indifference toward moral, artistic, and scientific values.

The most essential condition for the cure of our society is the abandonment of political persecution, in its judicial and psychiatric forms or in any other form of which our bureaucratic and bigoted system, with its totalitarian interference by the state in the lives of the citizens, is capable, such as dismissal from work, expulsion from college, refusal of residence permits, limitation of promotion at work, etc.

The first beginnings of a moral regeneration of the people and the intelligentsia, which resulted from the curbing of the most extreme manifestations of the Stalinist system of blind terror, met with no proper understanding in ruling circles. The basic class, social, and ideological features of the regime did not undergo any essential change. With pain and alarm I have to note that after a period of largely illusory liberalism there is once again an extension of restrictions on ideological freedom, efforts to suppress information not controlled by the state, fresh persecution for political and ideological reasons and a deliberate aggravation of nationalities problems. The fifteen months since the submission of the memorandum have brought new and disturbing evidence about the development of these tendencies.

The wave of political arrests in the first few months of 1972 is particularly alarming. Numerous arrests took place in Ukraine. Arrests have also taken place in Moscow, Leningrad, and other regions of the country.

The attention of the public has also been drawn during these months to the trial of Bukovsky in Moscow and of Strokatova in Odessa, and other trials. The use of psychiatry for political purposes is fraught with extremely dangerous consequences for society and constitutes a completely inadmissible interference with basic human rights. There have been numerous protests and pronouncements on this question. At present Grigorenko, Gershuni, and many others are being kept in prison-type psychiatric hospitals, the fate of Fainberg and Borisov is unknown; there are other instances of psychiatric repression (e.g., the case of the poet Lupynos in Ukraine).

The persecution and destruction of religion, which has been carried on with perseverance and cruelty for decades, has resulted in what is undoubtedly one of the most serious infringements of human rights in our country. Freedom of religious belief and activity is an integral part of intellectual freedom as a whole. Unfortunately, the last few months have been marked by fresh instances of religious persecution, in particular in the Baltic States.

In this postscript I am passing over a series of important problems that were dealt with in the memorandum and my other published documents – in the open letters to the Presidium of the Supreme Soviet of the USSR, "Let Soviet Citizens Emigrate!", and to the Minister of Internal Affairs, "Discrimination against the Crimean Tatars".

I also pass over the majority of international problems dealt with in the memorandum. I will single out from their number the question of limitation of the arms race. Militarization of the economy seriously affects international and domestic policy; it leads to encroachments on democratic rights, the open conduct of public affairs, and the rule of law; it constitutes a threat to peace. The role of the military-industrial complex in United States policy has been thoroughly studied. The analogous role played by the same factors in the USSR and other socialist countries is less well known. It is, however, necessary to point out that in no country does the share of military expenditure in relation to the national income reach such proportions as in the USSR (over 40 percent). In an atmosphere of mutual suspicion the problem of control mentioned in the memorandum assumes a special role.

I write this postscript a short time after the signing of important agreements on the limitation of ABM systems and strategic missiles. One would like to believe that political leaders and the people who are active in the military-industrial complexes of the United States and the USSR have a sense of responsibility toward humanity.

One would like to believe that these agreements are not merely of symbolic importance, but will lead to a real curtailment of the arms race and to further steps that will improve the political climate in our long-suffering world.

June 1972 [23]

---

23. *Sakharov Speaks*, pp. 151-8.

Interview with Olle Stenholm

In late June 1973, Sakharov gave an interview to the Swedish journalist, Olle Stenholm, which was broadcast in Sweden on 2 July 1973. Sakharov writes about the interview and its consequences in his introduction to *Sakharov Speaks*.

> In the summer of 1973 I was interviewed by Olle Stenholm, correspondent for a Swedish radio station, who asked me questions of a general character. This interview had a broad response in the USSR and foreign countries. I received several dozen letters expressing indignation at the "slanderous" line I had taken. (It should be borne in mind that letters of the opposite kind usually do not reach me.) The Soviet Literaturnaya Gazeta *published an article about me entitled "A Supplier of Slander". The correspondent who had interviewed me and published his text without distortions was recently deprived of his entry visa and the possibility of continuing his work in the USSR. ... In this interview, as in the "Memorandum" and the "Postscript", I went beyond the limits of the subject of human rights and democratic freedoms and touched on economic and social problems, which generally speaking require special – and perhaps even professional – training. But these problems are of such vital importance to every person that I am not sorry they came up for discussion. My opponents were especially irritated by my description of our country's system as state capitalism with a party-state monopoly and the consequences, in all spheres of social life, which flow from such a system.*[24]

Excerpts from the Stenholm interview

Sakharov: In 1968 when I wrote *Reflections,* I was very far from the basic problems of all of the people and of the whole country. I found myself in an extraordinary position of material privilege and isolated from the people.

Stenholm: But, Andrei Dmitrievich, you are doubtful that anything in general can be done to improve the system of the Soviet Union, yet you go ahead acting, writing declarations, protests – why?

---

24. Ibid., pp. 48-9.

Sakharov: Well, there is a need to create ideals even when you can't see any route to achieve them, because if there are no ideals there can be no hope and then one would be completely in the dark, in a hopeless blind alley.

Moreover, we can't know whether there is some kind of possibility of co-operation between our country and the outside world. If no signals about our unhappy situation are sent out, then even the possibility, which might exist, cannot be utilized, because we wouldn't know what it was that needed to be changed or how to change it.

Then there is the other consideration – that the history of our country should be some kind of warning. It should prevent the West and the developing countries from committing mistakes on the scale we have during our historical development. Therefore, if a man speaks out, it doesn't mean that he hopes necessarily to achieve something. These are different questions. He may hope for nothing but nonetheless speak because he cannot – simply cannot – remain silent. In almost every concrete case of repression we really have no hope and almost always there is a tragic absence of positive results.

Stenholm: So – what is needed?

Sakharov: We need first of all greater openness in the work of the administrative apparatus. Quite possibly the single-party system is excessively and unnecessarily rigid. Even under the conditions of a socialist economic system a one-party system is not necessary. Actually, on some levels of the people's democracies, the one-party system is not needed. And in some of the people's democracies elements of a multi-party system exist although as a semi-caricature of the real thing.

We need elections to state organs with multiple candidates. In general, we need a series of measures that taken individually might have little effect but that in combination might shake the monolith we have created, which is so fossilized and so oppressive for the life of the planet.

The press must also change. Now it is so standardized that it has lost a significant part of its informational value. Facts are reported in such a way that they can be understood only by the initiated and that the picture of life in our country is distorted.

There is no variety in our intellectual life. The role of the intelligentsia in society is unjustly disparaged. Intellectuals are badly off materially even in comparison to manual workers. The disparity is much greater if you contrast our intellectuals' standard of living with that of intellectuals in Western countries that have reached a comparable stage of development.

The oppression of the intelligentsia has included ideological pressure, and an anti-intellectual atmosphere in the country, which denies teachers, doctors, and practitioners of other intellectual professions the respect they deserve. And anti-intellectualism has caused the intelligentsia to retreat into narrow professionalism, into a separation of their lives at work and at home. In the narrow circles of their own friends, people can begin to think for themselves and share different ideas. But this leads to increased hypocrisy at work and with strangers, and to a further fall in the morals and creativity. All this affects the cultural more than the technical intelligentsia. Our creative professionals feel that they have gotten into a blind alley. As a result, our literature is terribly grey, conventional and boring.

Stenholm: Permit me one last question. Haven't you ever feared for your health and freedom during the years when you've been so active?

Sakharov: I've never been afraid for myself, but that's partly due to my nature and partly because I began my public activities when I held a high position, so such fears would have been unjustified. But now I have reason to fear pressure directed not against me personally but against members of my wife's families. That is a serious and real threat, and I feel it coming closer. ...[25]

---

25. *Sakharov Speaks*, pp. 166-78.

Nobel lecture: Peace, progress, human rights

Sakharov was not permitted to travel to Oslo to receive the Nobel Prize in December 1975, and Elena Bonner read the lecture on his behalf. In his *Memoirs*, Sakharov says that he wrote the Nobel lecture easily and with enthusiasm – it expressed his views on peace, convergence, disarmament, progress, an open society, and human rights; it also captured some of his innermost feelings.[26]

Honoured members of the Nobel Committee, Ladies and Gentlemen:

Peace, progress, human rights – these three goals are indissolubly linked; it is impossible to achieve one of them if the others are ignored. This idea provides the main theme of my lecture. I am deeply grateful that this great and significant award, the Nobel Peace Prize, has been given to me, and that I have been given the opportunity of addressing you today. I was particularly gratified by the Committee's citation, which stresses the defence of human rights as the only sure basis for genuine and lasting international co-operation. This idea is very important to me; I am convinced that international trust, mutual understanding, disarmament, and international security are inconceivable without an open society with freedom of information, freedom of conscience, the right to publish, and the right to travel and choose the country in which one wishes to live. I am also convinced that freedom of opinion and other civic rights provide the basis for scientific progress and a guarantee against its misuse to harm mankind, as well as the basis for economic and social progress. They also constitute a political guarantee that makes the effective defence of social rights possible. In addition, I will defend the thesis of the primary and decisive significance of civil and political rights in shaping the destiny of mankind. This view differs essentially from the usual Marxist theory, as well as from technocratic opinions, according to which only material factors and social and

---

26. *Memoirs*, p. 433.

economic conditions are of decisive importance. (But in saying this, of course, I have no intention of denying the importance of people's material welfare.)

I should like to express all these theses in my lecture, and I should like in particular to dwell on a number of specific problems affecting the violation of human rights. A solution of these problems is imperative, and the time at our disposal is short.

This is the reason why I have called my lecture "Peace, Progress, and Human Rights". There is, naturally, a conscious parallel with the title of my 1968 article Reflections on Progress, Peaceful Coexistence, and Intellectual Freedom*, with which my lecture, both in its contents and its implications, has very close affinities.*

There is a great deal to suggest that mankind, at the threshold of the second half of the twentieth century, entered a particularly decisive and critical historical era. Nuclear missiles exist, capable in principle of annihilating the whole of mankind; this is the greatest danger threatening our age. Thanks to economic, industrial, and scientific advances, so-called "conventional" arms have likewise grown incomparably more dangerous, not to mention chemical and bacteriological instruments of war.

There is no doubt that industrial and technological progress is the most important factor in overcoming poverty, famine, and disease. But this progress leads at the same time to ominous changes in the environment in which we live and to the exhaustion of our natural resources. Thus, mankind faces grave ecological dangers.

Rapid changes in traditional forms of life have resulted in an unchecked demographic explosion which is particularly noticeable in the developing countries of the Third World. The growth in population has already created exceptionally complicated economic, social, and psychological problems, and will in the future inevitably pose still more serious problems. In many countries, particularly in Asia, Africa, and Latin America, the lack of food will be an overriding factor in the lives of many hundreds of millions of people, who from the moment of birth are condemned to a wretched existence on the starvation level. Moreover, future prospects are menacing, and in the opinion of many specialists tragic, despite the undoubted success of the "green revolution".

But even in the developed countries, people face serious problems. These include the pressure resulting from excessive urbanization, all the changes that disrupt the community's social and psychological stability, the incessant pursuit of fashion and trends, over-production, the frantic, furious tempo of life, the increase in nervous and mental disorders; the growing number of people deprived of contact with nature and of normal human lives, the dissolution of the family and the loss of simple human pleasures, the decline in the community's moral and ethical principles, and the loss of faith in the purpose of life. Against this background there is a whole host of ugly phenomena: an increase in crime, in alcoholism, in drug addiction, in terrorism, and so forth. The imminent exhaustion of the world's resources, the threat of overpopulation, the constant and deep-rooted international, political, and social problems are making a more and more forceful impact on the developed countries too, and will deprive – or at any rate threaten to deprive – a great many people who are accustomed to abundance, affluence, and creature comforts.

Sakharov ended his lecture by saying that we must fight for every individual person who suffers from injustice and the violation of human rights, and that much of our future depends on this.

In struggling to protect human rights we ought, I am convinced, first and foremost to protect the innocent victims of regimes installed in various countries, without demanding the destruction or total condemnation of these regimes. We need reform, not revolution. We need a flexible, pluralist, tolerant society, which selectively and experimentally can foster a free, undogmatic use of the experiences of all kinds of social systems. What is détente*? What is* rapprochement? *We are concerned not with words, but with a willingness to create a better and more friendly society, a better world order.*

Thousands of years ago tribes of human beings suffered great privations in the struggle to survive. It was then important not only to be able to handle a club, but also to possess the ability to think rationally, to take care of the knowledge and experience garnered by the tribe, and to develop the links that would provide co-operation with other tribes. Today the human race is faced with a similar test. In infinite space many civilizations are bound to exist, among them societies that may be wiser and more "successful" than ours. I support the cosmological hypothesis which states that the development of the universe is repeated in its basic characteristics an infinite number of times. Further, other civilizations, including more "successful" ones, should exist an infinite number of times on the "preceding" and the "following" pages of the Book of the Universe. Yet we should not minimize our sacred endeavours in this world, where, like faint glimmers in the dark, we have emerged for a moment from the nothingness of dark unconsciousness into material existence. We must make good the demands of reason and create a life worthy of ourselves and of the goals we only dimly perceive.[27]

Open letter to the President of the Academy of Sciences

These are excerpts from an open letter Sakharov wrote to the President of the Academy of Sciences from exile in Gorky on 20 October 1980. He received no response.

I consider it important to state my position on questions of principle and on the actions taken by government bodies in my case, to respond to certain public accusations, and to discuss the stand taken by my colleagues in the USSR and, in particular, by the Academy of Sciences and its directors.

---

27. *Alarm and Hope*, Alfred A. Knopf, New York, 1978, pp. 4-7, 17-18. © Nobel Foundation, 1975.

For two decades I worked as a scientist in the military-industrial complex and then, for more than twelve years, I have joined those persons engaged in a non-violent struggle for human rights and the rule of law. My life has forced me to devote particular attention to questions of war and peace, international security, international trust and disarmament, and their links to human rights and open societies. As my ideas evolved, they have often turned out to be unorthodox, at odds with the official line and with my own earlier opinions. My life, my goals and my ideals have changed radically.

Quite a bit earlier, I reached the conclusion that despite our people's passionate will to peace and the government leaders' unquestionable desire to avoid a major war, our foreign policy has often been dominated by an extremely dangerous geo-political strategy of force and expansion, and by a striving to subdue and destabilize potential enemies. But in "destabilizing" an enemy, we destabilize as well the world in which we live. ...

I am convinced that the prevention of thermonuclear war is our most important problem and must take absolute priority over all other issues. The resolution of that problem involves politics, economics, the creation of international trust among open societies, the unconditional observance of fundamental civil and political rights, and disarmament. ...

I oppose international terrorism, which undermines peace no matter what the terrorists' goals. States striving for stability in the world should not support terrorism under any circumstances.

A most important concept which over time became the keystone of my position is the indissoluble bond between international security and trust on the one hand, and respect for human rights and an open society on the other. That concept was incorporated in the Final Act of the Helsinki Conference, but words have not been turned into deeds, particularly in the USSR and the countries of Eastern Europe. I have discovered the massive and cynical nature of the violations in the Soviet Union of fundamental civil and political rights, including freedom of opinion and of information; freedom to choose one's country of residence (i.e., to emigrate and to return) and one's domicile within a country; the right to an impartial trial and to a defence; and freedom of religion. A society which fails to respect these rights is a "closed" society, potentially dangerous to mankind, and doomed to degradation. I have become acquainted with individuals who are using publicity in a struggle for human rights, who reject violence as a matter of principle. They have been cruelly persecuted by the authorities. I have been an eyewitness to unjust trials. I have seen the brazen, crude acts of the KGB. I have learned about terrible conditions in places of detention. I have become one of those people you have called an "alien clique" and have even been accused of treason. They are my friends and they represent the shining strength of our people. ...

I have taken a fresh look at our economic difficulties and food shortages, at the privileges of the bureaucratic and Party elite, at the stagnation of our industry, at the menacing signs of the bureaucracy perverting and deadening the life of our entire country, at the general indifference toward work done for a faceless state (nobody could care less), at corruption and improper influence, at the compulsory hypocrisy which cripples human beings, at alcoholism, at censorship and the brazen lying of the press, at the insane destruction of the environment, the soil, air, forests, rivers and lakes. The necessity for profound economic and social reforms in the USSR is obvious, but attempts to implement them encounter the resistance of the ruling bureaucracy and everything goes on as before, with the same worn-out slogans. Occasionally something new is tried but successes are rare. Meanwhile the military-industrial complex and the KGB are gaining in strength, threatening the stability of the entire world, and super-militarization is eating up all our resources.

My ideal is an open pluralistic society which safeguards fundamental civil and political rights, a society with a mixed economy which would permit scientifically-regulated, balanced progress. Such a society should come about through the peaceful convergence of the socialist and capitalist systems. That is the main condition for saving the world from thermonuclear disaster.

The era of the Stalin regime's monstrous crimes represents half of the Soviet Union's history. Although Stalin's actions have been officially condemned, the specific crimes and the scope of repression under Stalin are carefully hidden and those who expose them are prosecuted for slander. The terror and the famine accompanying collectivization; Kirov's murder and the destruction of the cultural, civil, military, and Party cadres; the genocide occurring during the resettlement of "punished" peoples; the penal labour camps and the deaths of many millions there; the flirtation with Hitler which turned into a national tragedy; the repression of returning prisoners of war; the laws against workers; the murder of Mikhoels and the resurgence of official anti-Semitism – all these evils should be completely disclosed. A nation without historical memory is doomed to degradation.

I have expressed my views in articles and interviews which have appeared since 1968. Instead of engaging in serious discussion, official propaganda has deliberately distorted my position. It has been caricatured, reviled and slandered. I have experienced increasing persecution, threats directed against me and especially against persons close to me, and, finally, deportation without trial.

Yes I do live in better conditions than those of my friends serving long sentences or awaiting trial, among whom are many colleagues. I will mention only a few: the biologist Sergei Kovalev, the physicist Yuri Orlov, the mathematicians Tatiana Velikanova and Alexander Lavut, the young computer scientist Anatoly Sharansky, the physicians Victor Nekipelov and Leonard Ternovsky, the mathematician and computer scientist Alexander Bolonkin (all except Bolonkin I know personally). None of them broke any laws. None resorted to or incited violence. They attempted to achieve their goals through the written and spoken word. They acted as I have. It would have been only natural for the Academy of Sciences to have defended these repressed scientists. But my case is different in that here the authorities abandoned even that poor imitation of due process which they have employed in persecuting dissidents in recent years. This is inadmissible both as a precedent and as a relapse. Not a single one of the official institutions charged with executing the law accepted the responsibility for my banishment. According to generally accepted legal principles only a court can determine a person's guilt and punishment. My case is an example of flagrant lawlessness and thus my demand for an open trial is a profoundly serious and principled demand. I am not asking for mercy – I am demanding justice. ...

Prior to the General Meeting of Soviet Academy of Sciences in March 1980, I requested the Presidium of the Academy to assist my participation in the meeting, which is my right and my duty according to the By-laws. I received the reply: "Your participation in the General Meeting is not anticipated." The meaning of those words was underscored by the KGB agents who would not allow me onto the Gorky-Moscow train on the evening of March 4, the day before the General Meeting, when I was accompanying my mother-in-law and wished to assist her with her suitcases. The Presidium of the Academy allowed the KGB to interfere in the affairs of the Academy by formally allowing me to remain a member of the Academy but depriving me of a fundamental right of an Academician.

In sending you this open letter I am hoping that you will also reply openly, presenting your reasoned replies to the questions raised by me in this letter and, in particular, to the following: is the leadership of the Soviet Academy of Sciences prepared, in accordance with the wishes of the international scientific community, to actively defend my violated rights and the rights of other repressed scientists?...

The attitude of the Academy of Sciences and its leadership, not only in my case but in the cases of other repressed scientists as well does not correspond to the traditional understanding of solidarity among scientists. Scientists now bear great responsibilities for the fate of the world and this obliges them to remain independent from bureaucratic institutions, especially the secret police... I continue to hope even now that the Academy will display such independence.[28]

---

28. *A Chronicle of Human Rights in the USSR*, No. 40, pp. 21-4, 26-27.

Danger of thermonuclear war

Sakharov set forth in detail his views on the dangers of nuclear war in an open letter of 2 February 1983, to Dr Sidney Drell, Deputy Director of the Stanford Linear Accelerator Centre. He concludes his letter as follows:

In conclusion I again stress how important it is that the world realise the absolute inadmissibility of nuclear war, the collective suicide of mankind. It is impossible to win a nuclear war. What is necessary is to strive, systematically though carefully, for complete nuclear disarmament based on strategic parity in conventional weapons. As long as there are nuclear weapons in the world, there must be a strategic parity of nuclear forces so that no side will venture to embark on a limited or regional nuclear war. Genuine security is possible only when based on a stabilisation of international relations, a repudiation of expansionist policies, the strengthening of international trust, openness and pluralism in the socialist societies, the observance of human rights throughout the world, the rapprochement – convergence – of the socialist and capitalist systems, and worldwide co-ordinated efforts to solve global problems.[29]

The inevitability of perestroika

The Inevitability of Perestroika was Sakharov's last comprehensive statement in a series that began with his *Reflections on Progress, Peaceful Co-existence, and Intellectual Freedom*. It was published in March 1988 in *Inogo ne dano* (*No Other Way*), a collection of articles on *perestroika*, edited by Yuri Afanasiev and published by Progress Publishers.[30]

Our society has turned out to be seriously diseased. This did not come about suddenly; it was the result of a complex historical process. Its last stage has been called "the era of stagnation". The symptoms of our malaise are known,

---

29. "The danger of thermonuclear war," *Foreign Affairs*, summer 1983, Council on Foreign Relations, p. 1016.
30. This essay was translated by Edward Kline and is published in English for the first time.

and to some degree we understand its causes and internal workings, though we are far from a complete understanding of all its facets.

The first cause was the absence of pluralism in the government, in the economy (except for the period of the New Economic Policy[31]), and in ideology. The bureaucratization of the entire life of our country is closely connected with this. All the strands of administration have been concentrated in the hands of people who hold power because of their official position in the government or in the Communist Party, and who constitute a distinct bureaucratic caste. Bureaucracy is of course a necessary element of contemporary society, in fact, of any organized society. But several negative phenomena often appear in conjunction with its normal and often highly useful functioning: elitism; inflexibility, and an administrative command structure which strictly subordinates its middle ranks to the higher instances and completely disregards any democratic control from below, often with negative consequences. In the "anti-pluralistic" conditions of our country, these negative phenomena have acquired a qualitatively different and intractable character.

Stalin personified this new social force. This does not mean that the bureaucracy had an easy time under Stalin. In actual fact, his era saw the emergence of a one-man dictatorship, aggravated by Stalin's cruelty and other negative traits. Nevertheless, although other factors contributed to his ascendancy, Stalin had received his mandate to govern from the bureaucracy. This new power first showed its teeth by liquidating NEP, which could have served as the basis for a pluralistic development of our society in combination with voluntary co-operatives in the countryside and the rational growth of state-owned industry on a healthy economic foundation. But this pattern was unacceptable for the new Soviet bureaucracy.

---

31. The New Economic Policy (NEP) was adopted in 1921 in order to restore the Soviet economy after the Civil War by making concessions to private enterprise in agriculture, trade and industry. Stalin replaced NEP in 1928 with the first Five Year Plan, which called for rapid industrialisation. (Trans.)

What came afterwards is well known: forcible collectivization, the impoverishment of the peasants for the sake of hasty industrialization, and mass famine, with the appalling isolation of the regions condemned to destruction and almost no assistance for those starving to death. (This was just the time when our export of grain to the West peaked.) Then came the Great Terror, which devoured not only the Revolution's old guard and the military commanders but all the vital forces of our society, reaching its tragic apogee in 1937. And much more frightfulness followed.

* * *

The reforms attempted by Khrushchev and his aides were opposed by the bureaucratic establishment, the nomenklatura, and accomplished little. The economic reforms of the 1960s accomplished even less. These failures greatly influenced the psychological climate of the decades that followed. A further experiment with perestroika in the socialist camp was suppressed by tanks in 1968.

Nevertheless, after Khrushchev's condemnation of Stalin's crimes at the 20th Party Congress, the Soviet system rid itself of the extremes and excesses of the Stalin period and became more civilized, putting on a face that, if not entirely "human", at least was not that of a man-eating tiger. More than that, this new era was in some sense psychologically comfortable for many people.

But it was also a period of stagnation that led the country deeper and deeper down a blind alley. The possibility of expanding the economy by extensive means had been exhausted, and the system was incapable of growing by intensive means. As technical progress was not profitable for managers operating in a bureaucratic system, new technology was not applied nor was it even developed since bureaucratization also affected science. Many of our scientific and technical ideas have come from the West, often after a lag of years and even decades. For all practical purposes, our country has been dropping out of the scientific revolution and becoming its parasite.

Our productivity has fallen drastically. New construction is painfully slow. Mikhail Gorbachev's recent statement sums it all up: there has been no growth of our gross national product during the last four five-year plans, and in the 1980s, it has even declined. Our agriculture is in a state of permanent crisis, resulting in poor nutrition of the population, limited selection in food stores, and the necessity of purchasing grain and other agricultural products abroad. Despite all this, the bureaucracy strenuously opposes all initiatives seeking to strengthen the independent activity of the lowest links of the economic system and the material interest of workers in the results of their labour. A recognized example of this is the fate of Khudenko, one of the forerunners of perestroika, *who was accused of violations of financial discipline and sent to die in a labour camp.*[32]

Another aspect of our "era of the bureaucracy" is the moral degradation of society, which is itself closely linked to our economic deformities. Hypocrisy and lies flourish in the press, on radio and television, in schools, in the Communist Party youth organization (Komsomol), and in the family. Having been deceived so often by pretty words, people no longer believe in them. Our society is overcome by apathy. The stifling psychological atmosphere weighs especially on young people, alienating and corrupting them.

The bureaucracy is far from self-sacrificing. Concealing the realities behind demagogic slogans, our officials make a mockery of social justice in housing, in health care (most people, for example, have no possibility of getting up-to-date medicines), in the quality of education, and in people's material needs in general. The salaries of many workers, and especially those of teachers, doctors, and other rank-and-file intellectuals, have been artificially reduced,

---

32. From 1964 to 1972, Ivan Khudenko, an agronomist, was allowed to run a state farm in Kazakhstan with discretion to select his own staff and to decide their rate of pay. Productivity rose fourfold, workers' earnings eightfold, and the farm's income even more. At the instigation of the agricultural bureaucracy, a fabricated criminal case was brought against Khudenko and his experimental farm was liquidated. Khudenko was sentenced in 1973 to six years in a labour camp (where he died in 1974). He was "rehabilitated" in 1989. See Vaksberg A., *The Soviet Mafia*, St. Martin's Press, New York, 1991, pp 164-5. (Trans.)

in effect imposing a hidden tax that weighs most heavily on the lowest paid. The great majority of pensions are shamefully inadequate. At the same time, elite groups enjoy enormous, unjust privileges.

A social portrait of the era of stagnation would be incomplete without remarking on the colossal growth of various forms of corruption. Mafioso groups have sprung up, entwined with local Party and government structures, and with connections, as a rule, to higher-ups. The Uzbekistan mafia is a prime example, with its multi-billion rouble embezzlements, its inflated reports of the cotton harvest, its systematic bribe-taking, and its exploitation of the cotton-pickers. Thousands of people, children in particular, have become victims of the uncontrolled and massive application of defoliants and other toxic chemicals. Those who protested have been subjected to cruel punishments in underground dungeons and psychiatric hospitals.

In the Stalinist era, the forced labour of millions of prisoners, perishing in the terrible Gulag system, played a substantial economic role, especially in developing the sparsely populated regions of the East and the North. Of course, this system was not only infinitely inhuman and criminal, it was also inefficient, a substantial element in the wasteful extensive economy of that period, not to mention the far-reaching consequences of the barbaric destruction of the country's human potential. In recent years the use of forced labour for economic purposes has declined dramatically, but between one and two million persons are still in labour camps or fulfilling compulsory labour assignments.

* * *

Conditions of detention remain very grim. They fail to satisfy present-day standards and the demands of humanity. Prisoners suffer from unbearable labour, from inadequate food, from restricted visits (permitted extremely rarely, and then only with relatives), as well as from the whims of their keepers. Sentences are unbelievably long. In contrast to the Stalinist era, our prisons are now filled primarily with persons convicted of ordinary crimes, but it is important to bear in mind that our judicial and investigative systems are very primitive. (With the advent of glasnost *in recent years, information about this has appeared in the press.) The ethical conduct and legal knowledge of our judges are often quite poor. They depend for support on the local authorities. Their decisions often lack any explanation. They repeat the arguments of biased investigators, which are sometimes based on coerced confessions obtained by third degree methods. Moreover, our most dangerous criminals appear to be immune to prosecution, and some occupy high posts. The police, the Ministry of the Interior, the prosecutors and judges have turned out to be closely connected with this mafia in a number of cases.*

The world of the camps is the very bottom of our society. Their horror, the lack of any prospect for a brighter future, reflect the social tragedy and moral sickness of our life, as do the media reports about the awful conditions in our orphanages and reformatories. A disproportionate number of prisoners are products of our orphanages, and they tend to receive very severe sentences. It seems that such deprived individuals should be treated with special leniency, but in fact, the contrary often turns out to be the case. Former convicts also tend to receive unjustly harsh sentences. During the 1970s, I received hundreds of letters about these problems (and also about difficulties associated with emigration). Unfortunately, I was unable to help my correspondents.

* * *

As regards the KGB, in the 1970s and 1980s that organization recovered the influence it had lost in the 1950s and 1960s. But I should also note that the role of the KGB is not entirely negative.

On one hand, the KGB conducted a ruthless campaign of repression against the dissident movement that appeared in our country toward the end of the 1960s (or somewhat earlier). Though relatively few in number, it laid the psychological and moral groundwork for the pluralistic development of our society. I especially admire individuals who dared to act in defence of glasnost *and human rights, among them the editors of the celebrated* Chronicle of Current Events. *This typescript* samizdat *periodical appeared for more* than thirteen years (with one brief suspension). It informed the Soviet and international public about our unjust trials, psychiatric repressions, conditions in places of detention, and our country's problems regarding emigration, religious life, and minority nationalities. Other dissident groups were interested in particular issues, including some of the problems I have mentioned above.

Dissidents were harshly persecuted in the 1970s and 1980s, many of them spending long years in prisons, labour camps, and psychiatric hospitals. Some died in confinement, including Estonian scientist Juri Kukk, the remarkable Ukrainian poet Vasyl Stus, the Ukrainian teacher Oleksa Tykhy, and the worker and author Anatoly Marchenko. The misuse of psychiatry for political purposes was especially cruel and socially dangerous. (The danger was not reduced by the fact that many victims of psychiatric repression needed proper psychiatric assistance. It was in fact comparatively rare for a completely normal individual such as General Pyotr Grigorenko, one of the outstanding personalities of our time, to become the object of psychiatric abuse.) Justice requires me to note that the scale of political repressions during the era of stagnation was immensely reduced from the Stalinist era.

Did the KGB have links to the "Terrorist International," which appeared on the scene in the 1960s and 1970s, or to other destructive forces? This is an important question demanding a detailed and impartial investigation making use of glasnost and patterned on the US investigation of the CIA. I am convinced that our country needs to learn the full truth about our past and present, however difficult it may prove to be. There should not be any inaccessible corners of our life. (I am not, of course, suggesting the "outing" of our intelligence agents working abroad.)

On the positive side, the KGB, because of its elite status, was almost the only force untouched by corruption, and therefore a counterweight to the mafia. This ambiguity is reflected in the personal fate and position of Yuri Andropov, director of the KGB [1967-1982], who, becoming head of state continued to fight corruption and crime, but took no other steps to overcome the negative phenomena of the era of stagnation.

* * *

Examination of our international policies pursued during recent decades is also necessary. They too exhibited signs of stagnation, insufficient flexibility, and the absence of a truly fresh approach to today's unprecedented problems. ...

Trust in the USSR – and consequently, international security – has steadily declined. The noisy, often artificially instigated, "fight for peace" changed nothing in this respect. The USSR's involvement in Afghanistan has had especially serious, tragic significance. The introduction of Soviet armed forces met with strong national resistance, which the USSR countered with a cruel, multi-year war that has caused enormous suffering for the Afghan people. Somewhere between 600,000 and 1,000,000 Afghans have been killed. Hunger and disease are epidemic. More than 4,000,000 Afghans have become refugees, a quarter of the country's population. Many Russian soldiers have been killed or crippled. The waging of this unjust war has had devastating psychological and social effects within the USSR itself. The events in Afghanistan have become a major source of international tension and mistrust in the region and a threat to peace everywhere. The Afghan adventure embodies the whole danger and irrationality of a closed totalitarian society.[33]

* * *

I have outlined the stagnation and dead end of the mid-1980s. Fortunately, persons came to the fore who recognized that it was impossible for us to continue in this way. The slogans of perestroika and its ideology are well known: economic reform, glasnost, democratization (in particular, new principles for picking our leaders), social justice, new political thinking, and the priority of the common human goals of survival and development over particular state, class, ethnic, departmental and private interests.

---

33. Soviet troops completed their withdrawal from Afghanistan in March 1989. (Trans.)

Is the program of perestroika realistic? This is a question that interests everyone today. First of all, I want to emphasize that I am convinced of the absolute historical necessity of perestroika. And like war – victory is a must! But serious economic, psychological, and organizational difficulties and obstacles are inevitable. For many years, the people (and here I include the intelligentsia) have been schooled in pretending to work, in hypocrisy, lies, and egoism, in adapting to a corrupt system. Have they preserved within themselves adequate moral force? If this force is insufficient, then our progress will be slow and contradictory, with backsliding and reverses. But I believe that among the people, and among the young especially, a vital fire burns beneath their outer shell. It must make itself known. This depends on us all. Moral and material motivation is needed for perestroika. Each of us must be interested in its success. However, the sense of a great common cause cannot be instilled by decree or conjured up by pep talks, and yet, without it, everything will remain up in the air. The people have to believe that they are being told the truth. This requires our leaders to speak only the truth and the whole truth, and always to back up their words with deeds. Even in the most favourable circumstances, there will still be great difficulties. Already, the transition to enterprise self-sufficiency and self-financing, to new systems of supply, to co-operatives,[34] has cost many people part of their income, and some have even lost their jobs. And this is only the beginning of our difficult transition. It would be better, of course, if we can make fewer foolish mistakes and proceed in a more rational and responsible manner.

The main obstacles to perestroika are the ossification of the bureaucratic administrative system, which has grown with time, and its millions of employees at all levels, who have no interest in an efficient, self-regulating system. This creates the danger that some of them will actively, or passively, through lack of understanding or ability, hinder perestroika, will pervert it, will ridicule it, or will represent its temporary difficulties as its final collapse. We will have to get through all of this.

* * *

---

34. The so-called "co-operatives" of the late 1980s were in practice private businesses masked by a more ideologically acceptable label. (Trans.)

What more do I expect from perestroika*?*

First, glasnost. Glasnost *ought to create a new moral climate in our country. We have made great progress in this regard. There are now fewer and fewer forbidden themes. We are beginning to see our society as it was in the past, and as it is today. People should know the truth and be able to express their thoughts freely. Corrupting lies, silence, and hypocrisy should be banished from our lives forever. Only an individual who feels himself free can display the initiative needed by our society.*

A second, equally important foundation for society's moral health is social justice. I have already touched on the privileges of the elite, wages and pensions, social equality and certain other aspects of this broad, multi-faceted topic. ...

* * *

As I have mentioned, dissidents were subject to harsh persecution in the 1970s and 1980s. In the course of 1987 the majority of "prisoners of conscience" – persons imprisoned for their opinions or for non-violent actions in support of their beliefs according to Amnesty International's definition – were released. Some, including Anatoly Sharansky, Yuri Orlov, my wife and myself, were released even earlier. However, about twenty persons sentenced under Article 70 of the RSFSR Criminal Code remain in prison, labour camp, or internal exile, as well as some prisoners of conscience sentenced under other articles of the Criminal Code, or confined in psychiatric hospitals. All of them should be freed. This is critical for improving the moral atmosphere in our country and for overcoming "The Inertia of Fear".[35] *It is psychologically important that all prisoners of conscience should be rehabilitated, and not simply pardoned and quietly released. It is past time to end the practice of rehabilitating innocent people posthumously instead of during their lifetime. Furthermore, the 1987 demand that prisoners of conscience should formally*

---

35. The title of a *samizdat* book, published in English as: Turchin, V., *The inertia of fear and the scientific worldview*, Columbia University Press, 1981. (Trans.)

request a pardon was clearly improper from a moral and legal standpoint. All articles of the Criminal Code which were used to prosecute persons for their opinions should be repealed. This includes the above-mentioned Article 70, which is almost a word-for-word copy of the notorious Article 58 in force during Stalin's time. There is also Article 190^1 [circulation of fabrications known to be false which defame the Soviet state and social system]. Judges do not trouble themselves with seeking proof that the statements were "known to be false" or with analyzing the meaning of this phrase. In addition, there are Article 142 [Violations of laws on separation of church and state and of church and school] and Article 227 [Infringement of the person and the rights of citizens under the guise of performing religious ceremonies], which permit prosecution for religious practice. And, of course, the penal system should be made more humane and brought into line with international standards.

The complete abolition of the death penalty is also necessary. Beccaria, Hugo, Tolstoy and other writers and humanists of earlier times opened people's eyes to the extreme psychological cruelty of capital punishment. Besides, errors in court proceedings are inevitable, and they cannot be corrected after a defendant has been executed. The abolition of capital punishment would be a step toward the humanization of our society. Unfortunately, many people are not convinced of this, and, appalled by certain crimes, continue to campaign for its retention. I hope that their opinion will not prevail.

Perestroika *should promote the openness of our society as a fundamental prerequisite for the moral and economic health of our country and for international trust and security. The concept of "openness" should include: monitoring by society of key government decisions (repetition of a mistake such as the invasion of Afghanistan must be made impossible), freedom of opinion, freedom to receive and impart information, and freedom to choose one's country of residence and one's domicile within that country. All these points are contained in one of the most important documents of our time, the Universal Declaration of Human Rights, adopted by the United Nations in 1948, and also in the UN Covenants on Human Rights, ratified by the USSR* and referred to in the Helsinki Final Act. *Freedom to choose one's country of residence implies the right to emigrate and the right to return. The right to emigrate cannot be reduced to the reunion of families, and therefore the demand for an invitation* (vyzov) *from a relative – and still worse, from a "close" relative – is completely illegitimate. (Many applications for emigration have been refused on grounds of an insufficiently close relationship with the* vyzov*'s sender, and without a* vyzov, *there can be no discussion at all of emigration). In its most liberal form, the right of emigration has great social, political and international significance, permitting all citizens to choose the social and economic system, which they believe best for themselves. The borders between countries would disappear in some sense, and this would serve as an important guarantee of peace. A person's decision to emigrate should not, however, have a final, fatal character. People should have the option to reconsider their decision and to correct mistakes. The right to return is an important adjunct to the right to emigrate.*

* * *

I will proceed now to questions of peace and disarmament, which have been at the centre of my public statements since my 1968 essay Reflections on Progress, Peaceful Co-existence and Intellectual Freedom *published in* samizdat *and in the West. The* glasnost *era has allowed me to present my views directly to the Soviet audience.*

Taking a broader view, I believe it is practical and necessary for the USSR to consider a courageous step of extraordinary significance for people everywhere – a unilateral reduction of service in the Soviet army, navy and air force to approximately half its present length, resulting in a unilateral reduction of the armed forces, to be combined with a proportional, one-time reduction of all kinds of weapons. (The reduction of the officer corps should probably be smaller.) Naturally, such a decision can be made only after a complete review of all its possible consequences, including its effect on the military security of the USSR and other countries of the socialist commonwealth, as well as its social and demographic implications. It's also necessary to forecast international developments, including possible difficulties. But what weighs on the other side of the scales must also be taken into account! The proposed initiative would immediately and fundamentally change the whole international situation. It would open the way for all kinds of major disarmament, for balanced reductions of conventional and nuclear weapons, including the complete destruction of existing nuclear weapons. It would strengthen international trust. It would promote the resolution of regional conflicts on all continents. Disarmament will free up substantial material resources needed for perestroika *in the USSR, for solving social, ecological and other universal problems worldwide, for the struggle against hunger and disease, and for overcoming inequality in developing countries around the globe.*

The domestic social consequences of reducing the term of military service will be significant. It will facilitate young people's return to productive work and study. It will improve personal relations in the army – the basis for dedovshchina *[brutal hazing of draftees during their first year of service] will disappear. Reduction of the term of service is completely practical, since draftees today are much better prepared than the recruits of the 1930s; many are already familiar with tractors, automobiles, radios, etc. They can learn their military specialties in much less time.*

To retreat from the brink of global catastrophe, to preserve civilization and life itself on our planet, are necessary priorities for the current stage of world history. I am convinced that this can come about only as a result of profound geopolitical, social, economic and ideological changes leading toward convergence of the capitalist and socialist systems, an open society, and greater equality for all races and peoples, not only juridical, but also economic, cultural and social equality.

25 March 1988

Concluding statement to the First Congress of People's Deputies

Sakharov was elected to the First Congress of People's Deputies in April 1989. These are excerpts from his concluding statement to the Congress on 9 June 1989. Sakharov attached importance to this statement, which he reproduced in *Moscow and Beyond*.

I should first explain why I voted against the Congress's concluding document. It contains many theses that are correct and important, many ideas that are original and progressive, but, in my opinion, the Congress has failed to address the key political task facing it, the need to give substance to the slogan "All Power to the Soviets." The Congress refused to consider a Decree on Power, although a whole host of urgent economic, social, national, and ecological problems cannot be successfully solved until the question of power is decided. The Congress elected a Chairman of the USSR Supreme Soviet [Mikhail Gorbachev] on its very first day, without a broad political discussion and without even a token alternative. In my opinion, the Congress committed a serious mistake that will significantly reduce its ability to influence national policy and that will prove to be a disservice to our Chairman-elect as well.

The Constitution now in force assigns absolute and virtually unlimited power to the Chairman of the USSR Supreme Soviet. The concentration of that much power in the hands of one man is extremely dangerous even if he is the author of perestroika. *In particular, it opens the gate to behind-the-scenes influence. And what happens when someone else fills this post?*

The construction of the State has started with the roof, which is clearly not the best way of going about things. The same approach was repeated in the elections to the Supreme Soviet. Most delegations simply appointed a slate of candidates, who were then formally endorsed by the Congress, even though many of those selected are not prepared to serve as legislators. The members of the Supreme Soviet should quit their former jobs – but only "as a rule", and this deliberately vague formula has allowed the introduction of "wedding generals" [people invited to swell the ranks at a social function] into the Supreme Soviet. I fear that such a body will simply be a screen for the real power of its Chairman and the Party-state apparatus.

We are in the throes of spreading economic catastrophe and a tragic worsening of inter-ethnic relations; one element of the powerful and dangerous processes at work has been a general crisis of confidence in the nation's leadership. If we simply float with the current, hoping that things will gradually get better in the distant future, then the accumulating tensions could explode with dire consequences for our society.

Comrade deputies, at this moment in history, an enormous responsibility has fallen to you. Political decisions are needed in order to strengthen the power of local Soviet organs and resolve our economic, social, ecological, and ethnic problems. If the Congress of People's Deputies cannot take power into its hands here, then there is not the slightest hope for the soviets of Union Republics, regions, districts, and villages. But without strong local soviets, it won't be possible to implement land reform or any agrarian policy other than nonsensical attempts to resuscitate uneconomic collective farms. Without a strong Congress and strong and independent soviets, it won't be possible to overcome the dictates of the bureaucracy, to work out and implement new laws on commercial enterprises, to fight against ecological folly.

The Congress is called upon to defend the democratic principles of popular government and thereby the irreversibility of perestroika *and the harmonious development of our country.*

Sakharov appealed once again to the Congress to adopt the Decree on Power, which sought to democratise the exercise of power, including through the repeal of Article 6 of the Constitution, which stipulated that the Communist Party was the leading and guiding force of Soviet society, the nucleus of its political system, and of all state organisations and public organisations.

The Decree also sought to make the Supreme Soviet a working body of the Congress, and commissions and committees charged with drafting legislation responsible to the Congress; and to limit the functions of the KGB to those necessary for the protection of international security.

Later in his statement, Sakharov raised several other concerns that he considered the Congress should urgently address.

Now to ethnic problems. We have inherited from Stalinism a constitutional structure that bears the stamp of imperial thinking and the imperial policy of "divide and rule". The smaller Union Republics and the autonomous national subdivisions, which are administratively subordinated to the Union Republics, are victims of this legacy. For decades they have been subjected to national oppression. Now these problems have come to the surface in dramatic fashion. But to an equal extent the larger ethnic groups have also been victims, and that includes the Russian people, who have had to bear the main burden of imperial ambitions and the consequences of adventurism and dogmatism in foreign and domestic policy.

Urgent measures are required to deal with acute inter-ethnic tensions. I propose the creation of a new constitutional system based on horizontal federalism. This system would grant equal political, juridical, and economic rights to all existing national subdivisions regardless of their size or current status, and would preserve their established borders. In time, some rectification of these borders and of the composition of the federation will be possible and probably will become necessary, and this should become the main business of the Soviet of Nationalities. The Republics will enjoy equal rights, forming a union on the basis of a treaty providing for the voluntary restriction of each Republic's sovereignty only to the extent necessary for the conduct of defence, foreign affairs, and a few other matters. Differences among Republics in size of territory or population or a Republic's lack of an international frontier should not confuse the issue. Persons of different nationalities living together in one Republic should enjoy equal political, cultural, and social rights in law and in practice. The Soviet of Nationalities should be assigned the responsibility of monitoring this.

The fate of the forcibly resettled nationalities is a matter of cardinal concern. Crimean Tatars, Volga Germans, Meskhi Turks, Ingush, and others in this situation should have the opportunity to return to their homelands. The work of the commission organized by the Presidium of the Supreme Soviet to deal with the question of the Crimean Tatars has clearly been unsatisfactory.

Religious problems are closely associated with national problems. Any infringement of freedom of conscience is impermissible. It is intolerable that the Ukrainian Catholic church has still not been officially recognized.

The most urgent political question is the confirmation of the role of the soviets and their independence. The elections of soviets at all levels must be conducted by genuinely democratic methods. The electoral law should be amended based on the experience of elections to the Congress. Regional meetings [to screen candidates] should be eliminated, and all candidates should have equal access to the mass media.

The Congress should adopt, in my opinion, a resolution embodying the principles of the Rule of Law. These principles include: freedom of speech and conscience; the possibility for private citizens and public organizations to contest before an independent tribunal the acts and decisions of all officials and government agencies; due process in trial and investigatory procedure (access to defence counsel from the very beginning of a criminal investigation; trial by jury; transfer of jurisdiction over criminal investigations from the Procurator's office, which should be solely concerned with faithful execution of the laws).

I urge that the laws on meetings and demonstrations and on the use of internal troops be reviewed, and that the Decree of April 8 [on subversion and the defamation of state organs] not be confirmed.

The Congress does not have the power instantaneously to feed the country, instantaneously to solve our nationality problems, instantaneously to eliminate the budget deficit, instantaneously to make the air and water and woods clean again, but what we are obliged to do is to establish political guarantees that these problems will be solved. That is what our country expects from us.[36]

---

36. The full text of Sakharov's final appeal to the congress, including his Decree on Power, is included in *Moscow and Beyond*, pp. 150-6.

III. Human rights activities

In an autobiographical note written in 1974, Sakharov gave a partial answer to the question as to why he had turned from worldwide problems to the defence of individual people.

> *I am convinced that under the conditions obtaining in our country a position based on morality and law is the most correct one, as corresponding to the requirements and possibilities of society. What we need is the systematic defence of human rights and ideals and not a political struggle, which would inevitably incite people to violence, sectarianism, and frenzy. I am convinced that only in this way, provided there is the broadest possible public discourse, will the West recognise the nature of our society; and that then this struggle will become part of a worldwide movement for the salvation of all mankind.*[37]

The writings in this section shed light on the activities of Sakharov and of the civic groups that emerged in the Soviet Union and Eastern Europe in the 1960s with a common commitment to uphold and defend human rights. Sakharov's own engagement intensified after his departure from Arzamas-16 in 1968. In 1970 he co-founded – with two young physicists – the Moscow Human Rights Committee.

The section begins with excerpts from "The Responsibility of Scientists", which Sakharov lists in his *Memoirs* as one of six important statements that he wrote in exile. It ends with actions he took on questions that remain relevant today: the rehabilitation of Stalin; prisoners of conscience and political prisoners; political trials; the rule of law; capital punishment; and protection of the environment.

In 1966 I sent a telegram to the Supreme Soviet about a new law, then being drafted, which would facilitate prosecutions for one's opinions (Article 190^1 of the Criminal Code). Thus for the first time my own fate became intertwined with the

---

37. *Sakharov Speaks*, p. 44.

fate of that group of people – a group that was small but carried great weight on the moral (and, I dare say, the historical) plane – who subsequently came to be called "dissidents." (Personally, I am fonder of the old Russian word "free-thinkers" – volnomyslyashchie). Very shortly thereafter, I had occasion to write a letter to Brezhnev protesting the arrest of four of them: Alexander Ginzburg, Yuri Galanskov (who perished tragically in a camp in 1972), Vera Lashkova, and Alexei Dobrovolsky. In connection with this letter and my previous actions, the minister heading up the department for which I worked said of me: Sakharov is an outstanding scientist and we have rewarded him well, but he's "a stupid politician."[38]

The responsibility of scientists

Sakharov wrote this essay for an international conference held in honour of his 60th birthday in New York on 1-2 May 1981.

Because of the international nature of our profession, scientists form the one real worldwide community which exists today. There is no doubt about this with respect to the substance of science: Schrodinger's equation and the formula $E = mc^2$ are equally valid on all continents. But the integration of the scientific community has inevitably progressed beyond narrow professional interests and now embraces a broad range of universal issues, including ethical questions. And I believe this trend should and will continue.

Scientists, engineers, and other specialists derive from their professional knowledge and the advantages of their occupations a broad and deep understanding of the potential benefits – but also the risks – entailed in the application of science and technology. They also develop an awareness of the positive and negative tendencies of progress generally, and its possible consequences.

---

38. *Sakharov Speaks*, p. 36.

Colossal opportunities exist for the application of recent advances in physics, chemistry, and biochemistry; technology and engineering; computer science; medicine and genetics; physiology and hygiene; microbiology (including industrial microbiology); industrial and agricultural management techniques; psychology; and other exact and social sciences. And we can anticipate more achievements to come. We all share the responsibility to work for the full realization of the results of scientific research in a world where most people's lives have become more difficult, where so many are threatened by hunger, premature illness, and untimely death.

But scientists and scholars cannot fail to think about the dangers stemming from uncontrolled progress, from unregulated industrial development, and especially from military applications of scientific achievements. There has been public discussion of topics related to scientific progress: nuclear power; the population explosion; genetic engineering; regulation of industry to protect the environment; protection of air quality, of flora and fauna, and of rivers, lakes, seas, and oceans; the impact of mass media. Unfortunately, despite the urgent and serious nature of the issues at stake, such discussions are often uninformed, prejudiced, or politicized, and sometimes simply dishonest. Experts, therefore, are under an obligation to subject these problems to unbiased and searching examination, making all socially significant information available to the public in direct, firsthand form, and not just in filtered versions. ...

With some important exceptions (primarily affecting totalitarian countries), scientists are not only better informed than the average person, but also strive for and enjoy more independence and freedom. Freedom, however, always entails responsibility. Scientists and other experts already influence or have the capacity to influence public opinion and their governments. (That influence should not be exaggerated, but it is substantial.) My view of the situation of scientists in the contemporary world has convinced me that they have special professional and social responsibilities. It is often difficult to separate one from the other – the communication of information, the popularization of scientific knowledge, and the publication of endorsements or warnings are examples of activities with both professional and social aspects. …

Another subject which is closely connected to questions of peace, trust, and understanding among countries is the international defence of human rights. Freedom of opinion, freedom to exchange information, and freedom of movement are necessary for true accountability of the authorities, which in turn prevents abuses of power in domestic and international matters. I believe that such accountability would make impossible tragic mistakes like the Soviet invasion of Afghanistan and would inhibit manifestations of an expansionist foreign policy and acts of internal repression.

The unrestricted sale of newspapers, magazines, and books published abroad would be a major step toward effective freedom of information in totalitarian countries. Perhaps even more significant would be the abolition of censorship which should concern first of all the scientists and intelligentsia of totalitarian countries. It is important to demand a halt to jamming of foreign broadcasts which deprives millions of access to the uncensored information needed to form an independent judgment of events. (Jamming was resumed in the USSR in August 1980 after a seven-year interval.)

I am convinced that support of Amnesty International's call for a general, worldwide amnesty for prisoners of conscience is of special importance. The political amnesties proclaimed by a number of countries in recent years have helped to improve the atmosphere. An amnesty for prisoners of conscience in the USSR, in Eastern Europe, and in all other countries where political prisoners or prisoners of conscience are detained would not only be of major humanitarian significance but could also enhance international confidence and security.

The worldwide character of the scientific community assumes particular importance when dealing with such problems. By its international defence of persecuted scientists and of all persons whose rights have been violated, the scientific community confirms its international mandate which is so essential for successful scientific work and for service to society.

Western scientists are familiar with the names of many Soviet colleagues who have been subjected to unlawful repressions. (I shall confine my discussion to the Soviet Union, since I am better informed about it, but serious human rights violations occur in other countries, including those of Eastern Europe.) The individuals I mention have neither advocated nor used violence, since they consider publicity the only acceptable, effective, and non-pernicious way of defending human rights. Thus, they are all prisoners of conscience as defined by Amnesty International. Their stories have much else in common. Their trials were conducted in flagrant violation of statutory procedures and in defiance of elementary common sense. ...

In the labour camps, prisoners of conscience suffer cruel treatment: arbitrary confinement in punishment cells; torture by cold and hunger; infrequent family visits subject to capricious cancellation; and similar restrictions on correspondence. They share all the rigours of the Soviet penal regimen for common criminals while suffering the added strain of pressure to "embark on the path of reform", i.e. to renounce their beliefs. I would like to remind you that not once has any international organization, such as the Red Cross or a lawyers' association, been able to visit Soviet labour camps. ...

I appeal to scientists everywhere to defend those who have been repressed. I believe that in order to protect innocent persons it is permissible and, in many cases, necessary to adopt extraordinary measures such as an interruption of scientific contacts or other types of boycotts. I urge the use, as well, of all the possibilities of publicity and of diplomacy. In addressing the Soviet leaders, it is important to take into account that they do not know about – and probably do not want to know about – most letters and appeals directed to them. Therefore, personal interventions by Western officials who meet with their Soviet counterparts have particular significance. Western scientists should use their influence to press for such interventions.

I hope that carefully considered and organized actions in defence of victims of repression will ease their lot and add strength, authority, and energy to the international scientific community.

I have titled this letter "The Responsibility of Scientists". Tatiana Velikanova, Yuri Orlov, Sergei Kovalev, and many others have decided this question for themselves by taking the path of active, self-sacrificing struggle for human rights and for an open society. Their sacrifices are enormous, but they are not in vain. These individuals are improving the ethical image of our world.

Many of their colleagues who live in totalitarian countries but who have not found within themselves the strength for such struggle do try to fulfil honestly their professional responsibilities. It is, in fact, essential to work at one's profession. But has not the time come for those scientists, who often exhibit their perception and non-conformity when with close friends, to demonstrate their sense of responsibility in some fashion which has more social significance, and to take a more public stand, at least on issues such as the defence of their persecuted colleagues and control over the faithful execution of domestic laws and the performance of international obligations? Every true scientist should undoubtedly muster sufficient courage and integrity to resist the temptation and the habit of conformity. Unfortunately, we are familiar with too many counter-examples in the Soviet Union, sometimes using the excuse of protecting one's laboratory or institute (usually just a pretext), sometimes for the sake of one's career, sometimes for the sake of foreign travel (a major lure in a closed country such as ours). ...

Western scientists face no threat of prison or labour camp for public stands; they cannot be bribed by an offer of foreign travel to forsake such activity. But this in no way diminishes their responsibility. Some Western intellectuals warn against social involvement as a form of politics. But I am not speaking about a struggle for power – it is not politics. It is a struggle to preserve peace and those ethical values which have been developed as our civilization evolved. By their example and by their fate, prisoners of conscience affirm that the defence of justice, the international defence of individual victims of violence, the defence of mankind's lasting interests are the responsibility of every scientist.

Gorky, 24 March 1981[39]

Eastern Europe

Sakharov gave the following interview to a correspondent from the Italian newspaper, *Corriere della Sera* on 26 January 1977.

Sakharov: All of us in the USSR feel great admiration for the new escalation of activity on the part of our East European friends – the organizers of Charter 77 in Czechoslovakia, the Workers' Defence Committee in Poland, and others. We will never forget the role of the Prague Spring of 1968 in the formation of the human rights movement in the USSR.

Q: Do you think that links between Soviet and East European dissidents will form in the future?

Sakharov: One of the fundamental features of totalitarian societies is that information exchange is blocked both within a country and across its borders. Only monumental efforts (and sometimes even sacrifice) have made it possible to maintain as much contact with Western countries as there is now; any slackening in attention to this problem threatens the gains already achieved. Other dissidents and I cannot pick up a telephone and call our friends in Eastern Europe; nor can we write them letters. Of course, we would all like to have free personal contact, or even better, the opportunity to issue joint statements, as well as less formal means of co-ordinating our efforts. Perhaps international support will someday provide us with such opportunities – which would be important not only

---

39. *On Sakharov*, pp. 205-11. English translation courtesy of Khronika Press.

for our countries. But nevertheless, it is my feeling now that even at a distance we have a definite, albeit incomplete, understanding of one another, a feeling of touching elbows.

Q: How do you assess Charter 77 and the official Soviet reaction to it?

Sakharov: I see Charter 77 as a historic document representing an important new step in the struggle for human rights not only in Czechoslovakia but in all Communist countries. It is of special relevance that Charter 77 bases itself on the most important international documents – the Universal Declaration of Human Rights; the International Covenant on Human Rights, which has the force of law; and the Helsinki Final Act – and illustrates the discrepancies between the real situation and the principles these documents promote. The very spirit of Charter 77, its restrained pathos and force, evoke great sympathy in me. The fact that this document was signed by three hundred Czechoslovak citizens and, without doubt, supported by many others throughout the country, was the factor which provoked the authorities' rage and made them organize false spectacles of public censure.

The Soviet press reaction to Charter 77 is very significant. It poses a threat not only to Czechoslovak, but to Soviet dissidents. As usual, of course, Charter 77 itself was never published or even quoted, a fact which simply shows how incapable official propaganda is of waging an honest, open struggle of ideas on any sort of equal ground.

Q: Do you think that this document could be accepted by Soviet dissidents?

Sakharov: I think it could. The whole spirit of the document is undoubtedly close to Soviet dissidents. As for me, if Charter 77 were to grant citizens of other countries the right to sign it, I would request that my signature, and that of my wife, Elena Bonner, be added to this statement.

Q: What type of aid can dissidents in the USSR and Eastern Europe expect from Western Communist parties?

Sakharov: The dissident movements, or, to be exact, the human rights movements in our countries, are not political in nature. Their participants hold divergent views of the world. We feel that our movements are of significance not only for the future of our countries, but for all of mankind. We rely on the support of all honest, humane, and farsighted people throughout the world, regardless of their political platform.

We have a special need for open discussion, for widespread and objective publicity concerning the real facts about our countries, facts undistorted by official propaganda. If the Communist press were to report such facts – in particular, to speak in defence of political prisoners and freedom of conscience, to foster information exchange, and uphold the free flow of people – it would make an important contribution to our human rights movements.[40]

The human rights movement in the USSR

Sakharov provided the following response to questions from a journalist on 22 February 1980, one month after he was exiled to Gorky.

The moral significance of the human rights movement, which arose in the middle of the 1960s, has been enormous, although the movement itself is small in number and deliberately apolitical. It has changed the moral climate and created the spiritual preconditions for democratic changes in the USSR and for the formulation of an ideology of human rights throughout the world. Dangerous illusions about our system, which used to be almost universal among Western intellectuals, have almost disappeared. I myself felt the attraction of the human rights movement in the mid-1960s. It deeply affected my attitudes and my public activities.

---

40. *Alarm and Hope*, pp. 139-43.

I don't think that many human rights advocates expected that the regime would recognize the justice of our appeals. The fact that we addressed the authorities was simply a natural reflection of our aspiration for a rule of law, of our loyalty to the state, of our confidence that we were in the right legally as well as ethically. People might have hoped that there might be results in certain cases for specific individuals. That is, however, different from changes in the regime's policies.

I don't believe the regime was frightened by radical demands. The main body of dissidents was hardly radical: does a request to allow Tatars to return to the Crimea or to release someone from a psychiatric hospital threaten the foundations of the state? The authorities simply opposed any display of independence or circulation of information from unofficial sources inside the country or to the West. But for our part, we could no longer live as we had in the past.

We enter the 1980s under difficult conditions. Exploiting the general aggravation of the international situation, the Soviet authorities have launched a major attempt to eliminate dissidence in Moscow and in the provinces. The attack is aimed against the whole human rights movement as well as against independent samizdat *journals including* A Chronicle of Current Events, *against the Helsinki Watch groups, and the associated commissions on the abuse of psychiatry and religious persecution.*

The persecution of religious believers has become more intense. Far fewer emigration visas are now being issued. Harassment of Crimean Tatars has been stepped up. ...[41]

Sakharov wrote again about the human rights movement in his *A Letter from Exile* of May 1980.

---

41. Sakharov's written responses, dated 22 February 1980, to the questions of Kevin Klose, a correspondent of the *Washington Post*, were published in the *Washington Post*, 9 March 1980.

The human rights movement has no political objectives and its participants have no desire to gain political power. Their only weapon is free access to and dissemination of information. It is of vital importance that the movement limit itself to non-violent methods. Such a position is logical in a country that has passed through the violence of every circle of hell. Calls for new revolutionary upheavals or for intervention would be mad, and a terrible crime in an unstable world only several steps from the thermonuclear abyss.

Participants in the human rights movement speak out openly for human rights whenever they learn of violations, and they inform the public. They have also set themselves the task of correcting the historical record about our society and its individual citizens where the truth has been distorted by official propaganda. They help the families of victims of repression. I am convinced that this is what is needed – a pure moral movement to plant in people's minds a basis for democratic and pluralist transformation. This is crucial for our country and the world and for the sake of peace on earth. ...

A nation that has suffered the horrible losses, cruelties, and destruction of war yearns above all for peace. This is a broad, profound, powerful and honest feeling. Today, the leaders of our country do not, and cannot, oppose this dominant desire of the people. I want to believe that the Soviet leaders are sincere in this, that when peace is involved they are transformed from robots into people.

But even the people's deep wish for peace is exploited, and this is perhaps the cruellest deception of all. Their yearning for peace is used to justify all the most negative features in our country – economic disorder, excessive militarization, purportedly "defensive" foreign policy measures (whether in Czechoslovakia or Afghanistan), and lack of freedom in our closed society. And those negative features also include ecological madness, such as the destruction of Lake Baikal, meadows and fields, and the country's fish resources, and the poisoning of our water and air.

The people of our country submit uncomplainingly to all the shortages of meat, butter, and many other products – though they do grumble at home. They put up with the gross social inequality between the elite and ordinary citizens. They endure the arbitrary behaviour and cruelty of local authorities. They know about the beatings and deaths of people in police stations but as a rule keep quiet. They do not speak out – sometimes they even gloat – about the unjust treatment of dissidents. They are silent about any and all foreign policy actions. ...

The people of our country are to some extent confused and intimidated, of course. But there is also a conscious self-deception and an egoistic escape from difficult problems. The slogan "The People and Party Are One," which hangs from every fifth building, is not completely false.

But it was from the ranks of the people that the defenders of human rights emerged, standing up against deceit, hypocrisy, and silence, armed only with their pens, ready to make sacrifices, but lacking the stimulus derived from faith in quick success. They had their say. They will not be forgotten. On their side, they have moral force and the logic of historical development. I am convinced also that their activity will continue in one form or another, whatever the size of the movement. What is important is not the arithmetic but the qualitative fact of breaking through the psychological barrier of silence.[42]

A Chronicle of Current Events

A Chronicle of Current Events was a typewritten bulletin circulated in *samizdat* which meticulously reported and recorded the cases of individuals whose human rights had been violated. The distribution of each issue typically began with a dozen typed copies which recipients retyped and sent on in chain-letter fashion so that eventually the *Chronicle* spread throughout the country, creating a thousands-strong underground network which also functioned as

---

42. *A Letter from Exile* was first published in *The New York Times Magazine*, 8 June 1980.

a channel for gathering information for future issues.[43] Sixty-four issues of the *Chronicle* were circulated over a 15-year period from the first issue of 30 April 1968, compiled by the poet Natalya Gorbanevskaya, until the last, dated 30 June 1982. A 65th issue, prepared in autumn 1983, was never circulated.

The KGB vigorously pursued persons connected with the *Chronicle*. They were often arrested and charged under Articles 70 and 190[1] of the Criminal Code, with the courts handing down heavy sentences, as in the case of the astrophysicist, Kronid Lyubarsky, who reproduced and distributed copies of the *Chronicle*. He was convicted in October 1972 of anti-Soviet agitation and propaganda, and sentenced to five years in a labour camp. In late 1972, circulation of the *Chronicle* was suspended for fear of further reprisals against those associated with it. It reappeared in May 1974 with Tatyana Khodorovich, Tatyana Velikanova and Sergei Kovalev as its editors.

To tell the story of the Chronicle of Current Events *and of the people whose fate has been connected with it is a very important and difficult task. I have already repeatedly written – and it is my deep conviction – that the* Chronicle *during the course of these many years embodies the best in the human rights movement, its principles and highest achievements – the defence of human rights using objective information, and with a principled rejection of violence. The very fact of the almost uninterrupted publication of the* Chronicle *for almost 15 years is a miracle of self-denial, of wisdom, of courage and intellectual integrity. Undoubtedly people should know the history of the* Chronicle *and know at what price all this has been achieved. It is that lucid and bitter knowledge that both elevates people and makes them more tolerant, and more capable of making the right decisions in our beautiful and tragic world.*

April 1983[44]

---

43. See *1968 in Moscow* by Daniel, A., published by the Heinrich Böll Foundation EU Regional Office Brussels, May 2008. Edited by Nora Farik.
44. Andrei Sakharov's foreword to *Russia's Underground Press: A History of "A Chronicle of Current Events"*, Hopkins, M., Praeger Press, 1983.

Sakharov writes in his *Memoirs:*

> The Chronicle *avoided editorial judgments, concentrating on factual information concerning human rights violations in the USSR. Although the editors were working under exceptionally difficult conditions, they tried to be as accurate and objective as possible; errors were corrected in subsequent issues.*
>
> *It was essential for a journal of this sort to avoid anything that could be regarded as slander or subversion – and the* Chronicle *did in fact avoid such material. Nevertheless, its allegedly libellous character was used as a pretext to mete out exceptionally harsh penalties to anyone even remotely connected with its publication. Nothing frightened our security agencies more than those tattered, typescript bulletins – which only goes to prove the* Chronicle*'s significance and force. It was the clearest and most important expression of our human rights struggle and our only weapon – glasnost. The existence of the* Chronicle *for fifteen years was a miracle! The editors were anonymous, but it is now safe to honour the contributions of Natalya Gorbanevskaya, who is currently living in Paris; Tatyana Khodorovich, also living in France; Anatoly Yakobson, who died in 1978 after emigrating to Israel; and three who served long terms of imprisonment for their work on the* Chronicle*: Sergei Kovalev, Tatyana Velikanova, and Yuri Shikhanovich.*[45]

The Initiative Group for the Defence of Human Rights

The Initiative Group for the Defence of Human Rights was founded in May 1969. Some of its members were also editors of *A Chronicle of Current Events.* To mark its first anniversary, those members still at liberty issued an open letter in May 1970 explaining the group's purpose:

> *The purpose of our group is reflected in our name: the defence of human rights in the USSR. In calling ourselves the Initiative Group we also wished to make another point: To underline our right to freedom of association. The Initiative Group has no set program, no bylaws, and no defined structure. Each of us has the right to abstain from signing a document of the Group, and each of us has complete freedom when acting in his or her own name.*

---

45. *Memoirs*, p. 362.

The members of the Initiative Group have been brought together by certain common views. All of us – believers and atheists, optimists and sceptics, those who believe in communism and those who don't – are united by our sense of personal responsibility for everything that is happening in our country and by our conviction that recognition of the individual's innate value forms the basis for any normal life of a society. That is why we have adopted the cause of human rights. We understand social progress to mean an increase of freedom above all. We are also united in our determination to act openly, in the spirit of the law, regardless of our personal opinion of particular legislative acts.

The Initiative Group does not get involved in politics. We don't lobby for any specific government measures. We only say: don't violate your own laws. While we don't engage in politics, we have no intention of becoming reconciled to the punitive measures directed against dissenters. Resistance to illegality, to the abuse of power, these are the tasks of the Initiative Group. The Initiative Group does not believe that it is attacking the state when it criticizes specific actions of the authorities.

Some people, in the belief that protests harden the government's attitude and lead to more severe repression, criticize – while inwardly sympathizing with their views – those who speak out openly against illegality in our country. In fact, non-resistance, the humiliating submission to authority which implicitly sanctions violations of our rights, provides a fertile field for repression. Silence encourages evil and corrupts people, breeding hypocrisy and cynicism. Society needs glasnost. *Publicity inhibits tendencies toward extremism and violence of both rulers and ruled. In our country it is common to reproach anyone who appeals to foreigners. Unfortunately, no other means exist to publicize the violations of rights taking place in the USSR other than informing people abroad about them. News from abroad, even if only a little bit of it, reaches some Soviet citizens. And besides, we can always hope that our leaders will take international public opinion into account.*

We have appealed to the UN Human Rights Commission five times. The Commission has failed to respond to our appeals. Perhaps there exist reasons for this, which are unknown to us. In this letter we wanted to explain why we nevertheless do not consider our appeals to have been made in vain.[46]

The Moscow Human Rights Committee

Sakharov together with physicists Valery Chalidze and Andrei Tverdokhlebov launched the Moscow Human Rights Committee in November 1970. According to its Principles and By-Laws, both drafted by Chalidze, the committee would constructively study theoretical and practical problems in the human rights field, encourage knowledge of and respect for Soviet and international law, and advise individuals and state agencies on human rights questions. Sakharov writes about the committee and its beginnings in his *Memoirs*.

A few weeks before the Pimenov-Vail trial (October 1970), Chalidze had stopped by without notice, something he rarely did. He proceeded with great enthusiasm to outline on paper his idea for a Human Rights Committee, a voluntary, non-governmental association that would study and publicize human rights problems in the USSR. He was eager to announce the Committee's formation to the foreign press.

I was intrigued by Chalidze's proposal, despite certain misgivings. An independent association seemed an important and original idea, although it should be noted for the record that in May 1969 fifteen persons had organized the Initiative Group for the Defence of Human Rights and had addressed an appeal to the United Nations. The publication of A Chronicle of Current Events *and the founding of the Initiative Group had marked the emergence of the human rights movement in the USSR in the form that has attracted worldwide*

---

46. An open letter sent to Novosti and Reuters by eight members of the Initiative Group for the Defence of Human Rights on 20 May 1970, as translated in the appendix to Kline, E., *The Moscow Human Rights Committee*, unpublished manuscript.

attention – respecting the law, relying on public disclosure to achieve its aims, and remaining independent of the authorities.

I was uncomfortable with Chalidze's legalistic approach despite its merit, and I worried more that such a grandiloquently named Committee would attract too much attention and arouse too many false hopes. How were we to respond to the letters, petitions, and complaints that would come flooding in? That we were a study circle and not a defence committee? What a mockery that would be!

I expressed my reservations to Chalidze during that first discussion – they would prove justified a hundred times over. Much of the burden, moreover, fell on my shoulders, since people prefer writing to an Academician. Our conversation ended inconclusively, but the seed had been planted. ...

We formally launched the Human Rights Committee at an improvised press conference held in Chalidze's apartment on November 11, handing out copies of a news release to foreign correspondents who mingled with a crowd of dissidents. ...

The Committee met on Thursdays at Chalidze's. Although I didn't always understand the legal technicalities of the problems studied by the Committee, and was at times annoyed when Chalidze and Tverdokhlebov adopted what seemed an overly formalistic and needlessly paradoxical approach, I have never shared Solzhenitsyn's opinion that it was all a waste of time. The main thrust of the work contributed to the safeguarding of important human rights, and that outweighed my irritation with details. ...[47]

* * *

Over the years I have received a great many letters, some expressing support, others critical or even threatening. The KGB probably intercepted the majority

---

47. *Memoirs*, pp. 318-20.

of the sympathetic notes, letting only a small fraction get through. Hostile letters would appear sporadically; after receiving none for a while, I'd find bundles arriving, usually after I'd made some public statement. The threats were probably the work of the KGB, while criticisms of specific actions of mine may have been culled from spontaneous letters written by aggrieved citizens, and only in exceptional cases manufactured by the KGB.

Here, however, I wish to discuss the letters that asked for my help. These began arriving right after the founding of the Human Rights Committee in November 1970, the same period when strangers began appearing on my doorstep. In the nine years that followed until my exile to Gorky, I received hundreds of letters and visitors, each representing a serious problem that Soviet agencies could not or would not resolve. People would turn to me in desperation; right from the start, however, it was clear to me that I wouldn't be able to help most of them. It's difficult to convey the pain their misdirected expectations caused me; and, unfortunately, uncertain how to respond, disorganized and preoccupied with other urgent matters, I all too often chose the easy way out: I'd put off answering from one day to the next, from one week to another, until the letter was lost or there was no longer any point in replying. Still, my conscience was uneasy.

There would have been an even greater number of unanswered letters had it not been for the invaluable assistance of Sofia Kalistratova – a magnificent person, down-to-earth, just, intelligent, and good – a rare combination of the finest human virtues. For more than twenty years, Sofia, as a trained lawyer, had acted as defence counsel in criminal cases. She put her whole heart into her work, and her thirst for justice, her desire to provide her clients with both tangible results and moral support, never failed to move me. For Sofia, the fate of the individual was always the most important thing. ...

When Sofia agreed to help me with my correspondence, I brought her letters by the sackful. She would draft replies, explaining legal points, and offering wise counsel. I would discuss the letters with her and then sign them, and *she'd mail them. Sofia couldn't perform miracles, of course, and only in rare instances were we able to render practical assistance. But at least letters were answered.*

Sofia kept the letters and copies of our replies. The archive was confiscated by the KGB during a search of her home, so I'll have to rely on my memory in describing individual cases.

More than half my visitors were people seeking to leave the Soviet Union. ...

The second largest group among our visitors were those with grievances related to their jobs – conflicts with management, illegal dismissal, etc. Often, they'd gone all the way to the top in search of justice, with no success. At the USSR Procurator's Office, at the Supreme Soviet, and other government agencies, particularly dogged petitioners are directed to a special room and handed over to orderlies from psychiatric hospitals. In all honesty, however, I must say that some of those who brought their grievances to me were in fact mentally ill.

The stories of the elderly and disabled people who formed the third largest group revealed to me the hardship, often outright poverty, endured by those who depend on the social welfare system. Pensions in the USSR are for the most part extremely low, the exceptions being retired military personnel and a few other highly paid specialists. The elderly find housing problems particularly daunting. But there was nothing I could do in these cases.

Relatives of persons who had been charged with or convicted of crimes also came to us. (The vast majority of the letters I received were sent by prisoners or their families.) It was terrible to read in their letters or to hear directly from visitors tales of judicial errors caused by debased legal standards, of bias in trials and investigations, especially toward ex-convicts, of beatings and torture during interrogations, of arbitrary brutality in places of detention, of the judiciary's subservience to local party officials and the bureaucracy, and of the futility of appeals to the Procurator's Office or appellate courts, which barricaded themselves behind an endless series of form letters.

Some of my correspondents may have been guilty as charged, but these, I believe, represented only a small minority. The majority of the letters were too grim in content and too naive in style to have been invented.[48]

The committee prepared several studies and reports including on the right to legal counsel, the International Covenant on Civil and Political Rights and Soviet legislation, problems of civil rights in the USSR, the misuse of psychiatry and the rights of persons and peoples forcibly resettled during the Second World War. It also issued appeals.

The KGB kept the committee under constant surveillance throughout its existence. Yuri Andropov, head of the KGB, wrote in a report to the Central Committee of 1 March 1973: "The anti-social activities of the so-called Human Rights Committee decreased in 1972 as a result of measures taken by the KGB. These measures included compromising Chalidze's reputation, stripping him of Soviet citizenship [during his visit to the United States], and inciting disagreement and dissension among the Committee's members and sympathisers, which led to Tverdokhlebov's resignation." In a subsequent report of 15 March 1973, he reported that "The KGB continues to take measures to dissolve the Human Rights Committee and to contain the antisocial activities of Sakharov and his associates."

In his *Memoirs*, Sakharov writes that during 1973 and 1974, he, Podyapolsky and Shafarevich continued the committee's work, meeting regularly at his apartment on Chkalov Street, but although they managed to draft and publish several decent reports, they began to feel the committee had outlived its usefulness.

---

48. Ibid., pp. 501-4.

Valentin Turchin, Andrei Tverdokhlebov, and Yuri Orlov formed the Moscow Group of Amnesty International in October 1973. Tverdokhlebov was arrested in April 1975 and sentenced in 1976 to five years internal exile for defaming the Soviet social and political system. Orlov founded and chaired the Moscow Helsinki Group in 1976 until his arrest in 1977. Elena Bonner was a member. Sakharov preferred the freedom of speaking out as an individual, free of organisational constraints, while endorsing statements he agreed with.

After his return from exile, Sakharov was persuaded to join the Board of The International Foundation for the Survival and Development of Humanity, a US-Soviet initiative, launched in January 1988 to fund international projects and establish high-level working groups in the areas of environment, security, health, education, energy and human rights. He was made chairman of its Human Rights Committee, and organised a Human Rights Project Group under its auspices, composed of independent Russian and American advocates for human rights. Sakharov never felt comfortable about his participation in the Foundation, but the Project Group, with Sergei Kovalev as chair, did succeed in assisting the Human Rights Committee of the Russian Duma (1990-93), including drafting the Law on States of Emergency, reform of the penal system, and the Declaration of the Rights and Liberties of Man and the Citizen, the provisions of which were included in the 1993 Constitution of the Russian Federation. The Project Group worked with the Office of the Human Rights Commissioner (ombudsman) of the Russian Federation, while Kovalev served as Commissioner (1993-95).

The Memorial Society

In August 1988, Sakharov was elected a member of the Memorial Society's Governing Council. Memorial's purpose was to restore and recover the country's historic memory, focusing on the crimes and repression of Stalin's era. These were objectives that Sakharov fully shared and in line with his call in *Reflections* for meticulous analysis of the Stalinist past and its consequences, publication of the NKVD archives, the conduct of nationwide investigations, and the rehabilitation of the victims of Stalinism. Sakharov describes Memorial's difficult beginnings in *Moscow and Beyond*.

Earlier in 1988, I had been involved in the turbulent formation of the Memorial Society, another, much larger organization, with an uncertain but potentially substantial prospect of influencing public opinion. Some months before the Nineteenth Party Conference a group of young activists, including Lev Ponomarev, Yuri Samodurov, Vyacheslav Igrunov, Dmitri Leonov, and Arseny Roginsky called for the creation of a memorial for the victims of illegal repressions – at first, according to my recollection, they spoke only of a monument, and then of an entire complex to include a museum, an archive, a library, and so on. The idea quickly caught on throughout the Soviet Union, and a mass movement developed in support of the enterprise, which was expanded to encompass projects in regions other than Moscow, including the sites of Stalin's principal forced labour and extermination camps. In addition to its historical and educational tasks, the Memorial Society added the goal of providing legal and moral assistance to those victims of repression who were still alive.

Yuri Afanasiev presented a petition from Memorial with several thousand signatures to the Nineteenth Party Conference. The Conference authorized the erection of a monument to the victims of repression (a similar resolution had been adopted by the Twenty-second Party Congress in 1961 but it was never implemented); no mention was made of Memorial's other proposals. The movement began to organize, and a number of cultural unions, including the Cinematographers' Union, the Architects' Union, and the Designers' Union, as well as Literaturnaya gazeta, agreed to serve as sponsors. A bank account was opened for donations to the Memorial Society and for the proceeds realised from special concerts, lectures and films. At this stage, a poll was taken on Moscow's streets: passers-by were asked to name those they would like to see on Memorial's Council, and those who received the greatest number of votes were invited to serve on the Society's governing body. I was among them, and I accepted my nomination, as did the majority who received the public's endorsement.[49]

Sakharov writes that the Central Committee did not like the idea of an independent mass public organisation, one that would be hard to control and that contained many well known people among its members. It put numerous obstacles in Memorial's way.

> Memorial's status has remained shaky. The all-Union Memorial Society has been refused registration on the grounds that the only legislation regulating the registration of public organisations, passed in 1932, applies only to local organisations, not to national ones. All existing national organisations have been created by specific decrees of the government and purportedly do not need to be registered. Thus the Memorial Society still is denied access to its principal bank account. Some local chapters and their members have been harassed.[50]

Memorial was eventually able to register in 1990, after Elena Bonner urged Gorbachev to facilitate this when she spoke to him at the Academy of Sciences' funeral service for Sakharov. The Memorial Society and its numerous branches have played and continue to play a major role in the defence of human rights in Russia and the documentation of Soviet repressions.

Appeals and action

Sakharov was not a bystander. He acted when faced with wrongdoing. In the late 1950s, once he had understood their devastating consequences, he campaigned to stop above-ground nuclear tests. In 1964 he successfully contested the elevation from corresponding member to full member of the Academy of Sciences of Nikolai Nuzhdin, a protégé of the infamous biologist Trofim Lysenko. Appalled by the misuse of psychiatry for political purposes, he intervened in several cases of forcible confinement to psychiatric institutions, including those of Victor Fainberg, for participation in the demonstration of

---
49. *Moscow and Beyond*, pp. 57-8.
50. Ibid., p. 63.

August 1968 in Red Square against the invasion of Czechoslovakia; General Grigorenko, for his support of the Crimean Tatars; and Zhores Medvedev, for his activities against the supporters of Lysenko. Sakharov spoke out continuously on freedom of movement and freedom to emigrate at a time when those who tried to leave the country often faced arrest and imprisonment.

Over the years, Sakharov issued countless appeals and statements, observed many political trials, and even went on hunger strike when he could see no other way to achieve his goals.

> ... statements on public issues are a useful means of promoting discussion, promoting alternatives to official policy and focusing attention on specific problems. They educate the public at large, and just might stimulate significant changes, however belated, in the policy and practice of top government officials. Appeals on behalf of specific individuals and groups also attract attention to their cases, occasionally benefit a particular individual, and inhibit future human rights violations through the threat of glasnost.
>
> In dealing with civic issues and individual cases, it is vital that appeals be open. Private interventions are useful as a supplement – not a replacement – for public actions.[51]

Rehabilitation of Stalin

One of the first appeals Sakharov signed was a collective petition, dated 14 February 1966, addressed to Leonid Brezhnev, asking him to prevent the rehabilitation of Stalin. The letter was signed by 25 highly placed individuals, including academicians Artsimovich, Kapitsa, Leontovich, Maisky and Tamm, and writers Katayev, Nekrasov, Paustovsky and Chukovsky.

Dear Leonid Ilich,

Recently, in several speeches and articles, there have appeared tendencies aimed essentially at the partial or indirect rehabilitation of Stalin. We do not

---

51. *Memoirs*, p. 271.

know to what extent these manifestations have solid support behind them. But even if the only matter involved is a partial reversal of the decisions of the Twentieth and Twenty-second Party Congresses, this is cause for profound concern. ...

To this day, we do not know of a single fact or argument that would lead one to think that the condemnation of the "cult of personality" was in any way incorrect. On the contrary, one can hardly doubt that a substantial body of fact concerning Stalin's truly shocking and horrible crimes – information that would confirm the absolute correctness of those Congress decisions – has not yet been made public.

There is another issue, however. In our opinion, any attempt to whitewash Stalin entails the danger of creating serious fissures within Soviet society. Stalin not only was responsible for the deaths of countless innocent persons, our lack of preparedness for the war, the departure from Leninist norms in Party and government practice, but also by his crimes and misdeeds he perverted the idea of Communism so greatly that the people would not understand and would not accept any retreat, even a partial one, from the decisions concerning the cult of personality. ...

We are convinced that the rehabilitation of Stalin would provoke great unrest among the intelligentsia and would cause serious complications in the attitudes of young people. In view of our country's complex economic and political situation, it would obviously be dangerous to risk all this.

It seems to us there is another, no less serious danger. Stalin's rehabilitation is not only a domestic issue but an international one as well. Any step toward rehabilitating him would unquestionably bring with it the danger of a new split in the world Communist movement. ...

At a time when we are threatened, on the one hand, by greater activity on the part of the American imperialists, and, on the other, by the Chinese leaders, to risk a break or even complications with the fraternal parties in the West would be extremely unwise. ... A retreat from the Twentieth Congress would also cause great complications for our cultural representatives who maintain international contacts, especially in the movement for peace and in the area of international co-operation. ...[52]

This was a century of two world wars and many "little wars" which took with them many lives. It was a century of genocide such as history had not yet seen. A few weeks ago I stood together with five thousand of my fellow countrymen by an open grave in which victims of Stalin's terror were being re-buried. Representatives of three confessions stood by, administering the funeral service. There were Russian Orthodox priests, Jewish rabbis, and Muslim mullahs. The hundreds and thousands of innocent victims buried there included members of every nation and every religion.[53]

---

52. Cohen S. (ed.), *An End to Silence: Uncensored Opinion in the Soviet Union*, Norton, 1982, pp. 177-79.
53. *Andrei Sakharov: Science et liberté*, Les éditions de physique, 1990, pp. 17-18, on the occasion of Sakharov receiving an honorary doctorate from the Claude Bernard University, 27 September 1989.

Zoom on
Andrei Sakharov

1.

Cover: Sakharov, Moscow 1948. Photographer: D. I. Sakharov.
© Elena Bonner.
1. The Sakharov family, 1907. © Elena Bonner.
2. Sakharov (right) with mother and brother Georgy, Moscow 1948.
   Photographer: D. I. Sakharov. © Elena Bonner.

2.

3.

3. Sakharov with his father Dmitri, Moscow 1948 (photographer: unknown, but one of the family). © Elena Bonner.
4. Sakharov, his wife Klavdia and daughter Tatyana, 1948. © Elena Bonner.
5. Left to right: Yakov Zeldovich, Sakharov and David Frank-Kamenetsky, Sarov, beginning of 1950s. © Elena Bonner.

4.

5.

6.

6. With Elena Bonner at friends in Leningrad, September 1971.
   Photographer: © Radii Tsimerinov (St Petersburg).
7. Sakharov with Elena Bonner's family. Left to right, first row: E. Yankelevich
   (Elena's son-in-law); second row: R. Bonner (Elena's mother), T. Yankelevich
   (Elena's daughter), Elena, Sakharov; third row: A. Semyonov (Elena's son).
   31 December 1974. © Elena Bonner.
8. Sakharov at farewell for Pavel Litvinov in his parents' apartment. Left to right:
   Pavel Litvinov, M. L. Levin, Sakharov, S. A. Zheludkov, V. N. Voinovich,
   F. P. Yasinovskaya, V. P. Nekrasov, V. N. Kornilov, March 1974. © Elena Bonner.

9. Members of Human Rights Committee, from left to right: I. R. Shafarevich, Sakharov, G. S. Podyapolsky, Moscow, January 1973. Photographer: © Hedrick Smith.
10. Sakharov, Tatyana Turchin, Elena Bonner, Valentin Turchin, Spring 1975. © Elena Bonner.
11. Vilnius during the trial of Sergei Kovalev, December 1975. Third from right Efrem Yankelevich, fifth Sakharov, fourth from left: Yuri Orlov. © Elena Bonner.
12. Sakharov with Sofia Kalistratova, Moscow, 11 October 1977. © Elena Bonner.

11.

12.

13.

13. With Elena Bonner in Gorky, 25 October 1985 after Sakharov ended his hunger strike, Elena Bonner having received permission to obtain medical treatment abroad. The photograph was taken at a photographic studio.
© Elena Bonner.
14. At the railway station on the day of Sakharov's return to Moscow from Gorky, 23 December 1986. Photographer: © Yuri Rost.
15. Sakharov coming out of his apartment building, Moscow, July 1987. Photographer: R. Sobol.
© Elena Bonner.
16. Sergei Kovalev, Sakharov, Elena Bonner, Moscow, January 1988. Photographer: © Tatyana Yankelevich.

14.

15.

16.

17.

18.

19.

17. Meeting with President Reagan at the White House, Washington DC, 14 November 1988. © Elena Bonner.
18. Last day of First Congress of People's Deputies, Moscow, 9 June 1989. Photographers: V. Khristoforov and I. Zotin. © ITAR-TASS.
19. Sakharov at a meeting of the Interregional Group of People's Deputies, 14 December 1989. Photographer: © I. Zarembo.

20.

20. Funeral procession on the way from the Lebedev Physics Institute to Luzhniki, Moscow, 18 December 1989. © Elena Bonner.
21. Funeral: last tribute in Luzhniki. From left to right on the platform: Yevgeny Yevtushenko, Gavriil Popov, Dmitri Likhachev, Boris Yeltsin, Yuri Afanasiev; below: Dmitri Sakharov (Sakharov's son, next to the portrait of Sakharov), 18 December 1989. Photographer: © L. Sherstennikov.

21.

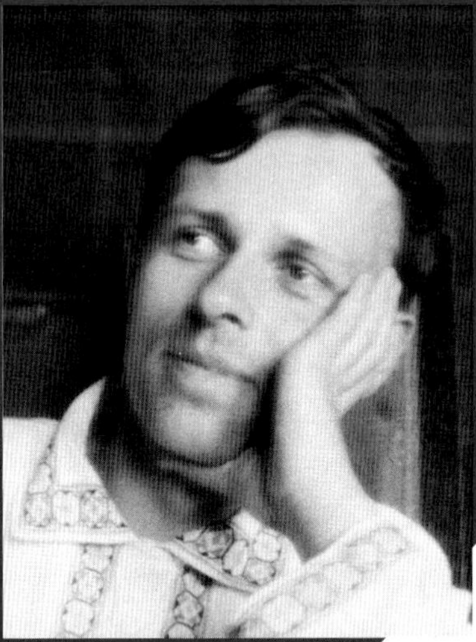

Prisoners of conscience and political prisoners

> *I am convinced that the defence of Soviet political prisoners and other dissenters, the struggle for more humane conditions in places of imprisonment and for human rights in general, is not only the moral duty of honest persons throughout the world but constitutes a direct defence of human rights in their own countries. But we often encounter a lack of interest in our misfortunes.*[54]

In early December 1966, Sakharov found an announcement in his mail box about a gathering in Pushkin Square on 5 December, Constitution Day, to observe a minute's silence to show respect for the constitution and support for political prisoners. A similar gathering had been held in the Square in December 1965 at the time of the Sinyavsky-Daniel trial. Such gatherings were to become an annual event.

I decided to attend. Klava didn't object, though she did say it was a strange thing to do. I took a taxi to Pushkin Square and found a few dozen people standing round the statue. Some were talking quietly; I didn't recognize anyone. At 6 o'clock, half of those present, myself included, removed our hats and stood in silence. (The other half, I later realised, were KGB.) After a minute or so we put our hats back on, but we did not disperse immediately. I walked over to the monument and read the inscription aloud:

> *I shall be loved, and the people will long remember*
> *that my lyre was tuned to goodness,*
> *that in this cruel age I celebrated freedom*
> *and asked mercy for the fallen.*[55, 56]

Sakharov then left the square with the others. He was later told that he was filmed by the KGB and that the footage was shown to high officials.

---

54. *My Country and the World*, p. 37.
55. Alexander Pushkin, "Unto myself I reared a monument," 1836.
56. *Memoirs*, p. 273.

Sakharov explains his attention to political prisoners in *Sakharov Speaks*.

> ... I should like to say a few words as to why I attach so much importance to the matter of defending political prisoners – defending the freedom of opinion. In the course of fifty-six years our country has undergone great shocks, sufferings, and humiliations, the physical annihilation of millions of the best people (best both morally and intellectually), decades of official hypocrisy and demagoguery, of internal and external time-serving. The era of terror – when tortures and special conferences [secret kangaroo courts] threatened everyone, when they seized the most devoted servants of the regime simply to fill the quota and to create an atmosphere of fear and submission – is now behind us. But we are still living in the spiritual atmosphere created by that era. Against those few who do not go along with the prevalent practices of compromise, the government uses repression as before. Together with judicial repressions, the most important and decisive role in maintaining this atmosphere of internal and external submission is played by the power of the state, which manipulates all the levers of economic and social control. This, more than anything else, keeps the body and soul of the majority of people in a state of dependence. ...[57]

In the autumn of 1972, Sakharov drafted and gathered more than 50 signatures on an appeal to the Supreme Soviet for a law on amnesty.

In the anniversary year of the formation of the Soviet Socialist Republics, we call on you to adopt decisions that correspond in their humanity and democratic thrust to the fundamental interests of our society.

We call on you to adopt, among such decisions, a law on amnesty.

We believe that this law should provide particularly for the release of those convicted for reasons directly or indirectly connected with their beliefs and specifically: those convicted under Articles 190^{1,2,3} and Articles 70 and 72 of the RSFRS Criminal Code, and under the corresponding articles of the Codes of other Union Republics; all those convicted in connection with their religious beliefs; and all those convicted in connection with an attempt to leave the

---

57. *Sakharov Speaks*, pp. 42-3.

country. We call on you also to review the decisions made on similar grounds to confine people in ordinary or special "prison" psychiatric hospitals.

Freedom of conscience and freedom to express and defend one's opinions are each man's inalienable rights. These freedoms are, moreover, a guarantee of a society's vitality.

We also consider that a law on amnesty, in conformity with juridical norms and humanity, should provide for the release of all individuals who have served a term of imprisonment in excess of the present maximum of fifteen years on the basis of sentences pronounced before the adoption of the Fundamental Principles of Legislation now in force.[58]

Sakharov issued the following statement on 4 July 1974, at the end of a hunger strike to call attention to the situation of political prisoners during President Nixon's visit to Moscow.

On June 28 I began a hunger strike as a protest against the harsh and unjust repressions directed against political prisoners, and in support of my appeal to the General Secretary of the CC CPSU and the President of the US.

In this appeal I urge amnesty for political prisoners and the immediate alleviation of the lot of those people whose sufferings are especially unbearable. I ask that the admission of international commissions to places of confinement in all countries be facilitated. I also call for efforts to foster realization of the right freely to choose one's country of domicile – a right which is central to international trust, mutual understanding, and rapprochement.

I am convinced of the importance of these appeals for the normalization of the world situation. My appeal and my hunger strike have been supported by many people in the USSR and abroad, and have attracted broad public attention.

---

58. *A Chronicle of Human Rights in the USSR*, Nos. 5-6, pp. 53-4.

For medical reasons, I have decided to limit my hunger strike to six days. This evening, I shall end my fast.

But it should not be forgotten that in Vladimir Prison, Vladimir Bukovsky is on a starvation diet in a punishment cell, suffering from dropsy. That in the Dnepropetrovsk Psychiatric Prison Leonid Plyushch is being tormented. And that after seven years of imprisonment, Igor Ogurtsov is languishing in Perm Prison, threatened with psychiatric reprisals.

I beseech world public opinion and all honest people not to relax their efforts in the defence of these people and in the defence of all others who are suffering so unjustly.

I hope that the leaders of my country will show good will and respond to these desires, beginning with the simplest thing – mercy toward those who are suffering.

I am deeply convinced that not only the spiritual health of mankind but its very physical survival depends on respect for basic human rights and on humanitarian principles.[59]

On 29 October 1976, Sakharov sent an appeal for a worldwide amnesty for political prisoners to Amnesty International.[60]

I call on you to raise your voices in defence of prisoners of conscience. Their suffering, their courageous, non-violent struggle for the noble principles of justice, openness, compassion, human and national dignity, and freedom of conscience, obligate us all not to forget them and to obtain their release from the cruel clutch of the punitive apparatus.

I will cite only a few of the better-known prisoners of conscience in my country, behind each of whom stand many more. They are Vladimir Bukovsky,

---

59. *A Chronicle of Human Rights in the USSR*, No. 10, pp. 21-2.
60. *Alarm and Hope*, p. 36.

Semyon Gluzrnan, Sergei Kovalev, Mustafa Dzhemilev, Valentin Moroz, Petras Paulaitis, Georgy Vins, Vasily Romanyuk, Danilo Shumuk, and Paruir Airikian. My friends at this meeting can tell you about their lives and achievements, but what I wish to stress is the tragic situation of each of them.

I call you to the fight for freedom for each of the political prisoners whose names are known to you, for the release of all political prisoners in the USSR, Eastern Europe, and the entire world.

I call for a general amnesty of political prisoners!

Amnesty International adopted Sakharov as a prisoner of conscience in 1980 when he was exiled to Gorky. In 1981, Sakharov asked the organisation to launch a special effort to win freedom for all prisoners of conscience, a request that inspired Amnesty International to launch a worldwide petition in December 1982, with Sakharov among the first to sign along with other Nobel laureates. Over one million people signed the appeal which was presented to the President of the United Nations General Assembly and the Secretary-General on 8 December 1983.

Thousands of men and women are in prison throughout the world solely because of their political or religious beliefs. Others are held because of their colour or ethnic origin. These are Prisoners of Conscience — none has used or advocated violence.

None of these people should be in prison. The fact that they have been arrested and punished because of their beliefs or origins is an affront to humanity. They should be freed unconditionally.

We call for a universal amnesty for all prisoners of conscience.

We believe that such an amnesty, backed by the United Nations and declared by all governments, is possible. It would give effect to the moral and legal principles of the Charter of the United Nations and the Universal Declaration of Human Rights.

This appeal extends to all those adopted as prisoners of conscience by Amnesty International and to those falling within its definition of such prisoners. The appeal will be presented to the President of the General Assembly of the United Nations and to all Heads of State.

In February 1986, Sakharov wrote to General Secretary Gorbachev from Gorky calling for the release of prisoners of conscience in the Soviet Union.

In February 1986, I wrote another letter to Gorbachev – it turned out to be one of my most important initiatives – calling for the release of prisoners of conscience. The immediate occasion was an interview with Gorbachev published on February 8 in L'Humanité, the French Communist newspaper: Gorbachev spoke about Soviet Jews, about Sakharov and – of greatest concern to me – about political prisoners. ...

Gorbachev had insisted: "Now about political prisoners, we don't have any. Likewise, our citizens are not prosecuted for their beliefs. We don't try people for their opinions." In my letter, after quoting those words, I showed that all prosecutions under Articles 70 and 190[1] of the RSFSR Criminal Code are in fact prosecutions for beliefs, and prosecutions under Article 142, which nominally deals with the separation of church and state, and Article 227, which deals with the "deleterious effects" of religious rites, are often similarly motivated. I also mentioned persons confined in psychiatric hospitals for political reasons and other imprisoned on trumped up charges. I gave brief accounts of fourteen whom I knew personally – Anatoly Marchenko headed the list – and called for the unconditional release of all prisoners of conscience.

The letter was mailed on February 19, 1986. I like to think that my letter, and my return to Moscow in the era of glasnost, may have played some role in the prisoner release program initiated in January 1987.[61]

---

61. *Memoirs*, pp. 607-8.

Political trials and the rule of law

In 1966 Sakharov co-signed a telegram to the Supreme Soviet on the addition to the Criminal Code of Articles 190^1 [the circulation of fabrications known to be false which defame the Soviet state and social system] and 190^3 [the organisation of, or active participation in, group actions which violate public order]. Co-signers included physicists Vladimir Ginzburg, Mikhail Leontovich, Arkady Migdal, Igor Tamm, and Yakov Zeldovich, writers Viktor Nekrasov, and Vladimir Voinovich, film director Mikhail Romm and composer Dmitri Shostakovich:

As Soviet citizens we feel it is our duty to bring to your notice our attitude toward the decree passed by the Presidium of the RSFSR Supreme Soviet on September 16, 1966.

> *In our view, the addition to the Criminal Code of Articles 190^1 and 190^3 opens the way to subjective and arbitrary interpretation of any statement as deliberately false and derogatory to the Soviet system.*
>
> *We are convinced that these articles are contrary to the Leninist principles of socialist democracy and that, should the decree be confirmed by the Supreme Soviet, they will constitute a potential obstacle to the exercise of liberties guaranteed by the Constitution of the USSR.*[62]

Their appeal was unsuccessful, and these articles were extensively used to clamp down on those who questioned the system, along with Article 70 which carried a harsher sentence, but required evidence of intent to harm the state.

The first of the many trials Sakharov observed was the trial of Revolt Pimenov and Boris Vail in October 1970:

I became even more familiar with the problems of defending human rights in October 1970, when I was allowed to attend a political trial. The mathematician Revolt Pimenov and the puppet-show actor Boris Vail had been charged with distributing samizdat – giving friends books and manuscripts to

---

62. Litvinov, P., *The Demonstration in Pushkin Square*, Gambit, 1969, pp. 14-15.

read. The items named in their case included an article by Djilas, the Czech manifesto "Two Thousand Words", Pimenov's personal commentaries on Khrushchev's speech at the Twentieth Congress etc. I sat in a courtroom filled with "probationers" of the KGB, while the friends of the defendants remained in a hallway on the ground floor throughout the trial. This is one more feature of all political trials, without exception. Formally, they are open. But the courtroom is packed in advance with KGB agents specially designated for the purpose, while another group of agents stands around the court on all sides. They are always in civilian clothes, they call themselves druzhinniki [auxiliary police volunteers] and they are allegedly preserving public order. This is the way it was (with neglible variations) in all cases when I was allowed to enter the courtroom. As for the passes enabling me to attend, they were apparently issued in acknowledgment of my previous services.

Pimenov and Vail were sentenced to five years of exile each, despite the fact that Vail's lawyer, at the appellate hearing, had argued convincingly that he had taken no part at all in the incidents incriminating him. In his concluding remarks Boris Vail said that an unjust sentence has an effect not only on the convicted person but also on the hearts of judges.

From the autumn of 1971 on I was outside the line formed by the druzhinniki. But nothing else had changed. At the trial of the well-known astrophysicist Kronid Lubarsky (who was also charged with distributing samizdat) a very significant and tragic show was put on. We were not allowed in the courtroom. And when the session began the "unknown persons in civilian clothes" used force to push us out of the vestibule of the court into the street. Then a big padlock was hung on the door leading into the people's court. One has to see all these senseless and cruel dramatics with one's own eyes to feel it to the fullest. But why all this? The only answer I can give is that the farce being performed inside the courthouse is even less intended for public disclosure than the farce outside the courthouse. The bureaucratic logic of legal *proceedings looks grotesque in the light of public disclosure, even when there is formal observance of the law – which is by no means always the case.*[63]

In December 1975, Sakharov travelled to Vilnius, Lithuania to observe the trial of Sergei Kovalev who had been arrested on 27 December 1974 for editing several issues of *A Chronicle of Current Events*. The trial took place from 12 to 15 December 1975, concurrently with the Nobel Prize ceremony in Oslo. Sakharov and other friends of Kovalev were not allowed into the court room. Kovalev was charged under Article 70 of the Criminal Code with conducting anti-Soviet agitation and propaganda. He was sentenced to seven years in a labour camp and three years of exile. Sakharov called a press conference on his return to Moscow on 18 December and made the following statement:

I would like to emphasize that Kovalev has been condemned because his conscience moved him to defend other people who, he was firmly convinced, had become victims of injustice. The charges against him – of seeking to undermine Soviet rule and of publishing libels – have not been proved. The trial itself was shamelessly illegal. It was closed to the public, and the accused was deprived of his right to a defence, including the right to defend himself and to make a closing statement.

Kovalev had been carefully preparing for a long time to refute the charges against him, especially those relating to A Chronicle of Current Events. *The seven issues of the* Chronicle *which figured in the charges against him reported on 694 incidents. The charges were based on 172 of them which had been investigated. Kovalev did not exclude the possibility of error in eleven instances, but intended to prove that none of these errors could be characterized as intentionally defamatory. Even the investigators agreed that eighty-nine reports were accurate, and Kovalev intended to prove that there was no error in seventy-two of the other investigated* Chronicle *reports. He was denied any chance, however, even to begin this task. It will probably be a long time before we will be able to read his doubtless well-founded and convincing arguments.*

---

63. *Sakharov Speaks*, pp. 40-1.

In court, the prosecution tried to use seven items to prove the charge of libel. Today we can assert that the prosecution managed to cast doubt on the accuracy of the Chronicle *reports only in one or two insignificant cases.*

The arrest and conviction of Kovalev constitute a challenge to public opinion in the Soviet Union and the world. After Helsinki and during the Nobel ceremony, the Soviet authorities clearly wanted to demonstrate their toughness and power, even at the expense of making a travesty of their own laws. To leave this challenge unanswered would betray a remarkable man and those central principles on which so much depends. The only possible response is to demand the annulment of Kovalev's sentence.[64]

Sakharov and Elena Bonner attended the trial of Yuri Orlov in Moscow, 15-18 May 1978. Orlov had been arrested in 1977 and charged with anti-Soviet agitation and propaganda. Sakharov writes in his *Memoirs* that many, himself included, thought the authorities would hesitate to arrest him, or that he would be sentenced to internal exile, but Orlov was given the maximum of seven years in a labour camp and five years' exile, and he was treated harshly while serving his sentence. He was deported to the USA in 1986 in an exchange, which also involved the American journalist Nicholas Daniloff, in jail in Russia, and Gennady Zakharov, a Soviet physicist and spy, in jail in the USA.

The many friends, foreign correspondents, and diplomats who travelled there were all barred from the courthouse; temporary barriers had been erected, and the police kept everyone at least fifty feet from the building. Orlov's wife and sons were allowed into the courtroom, but twice they were roughed up and their clothes torn in official zeal to prevent them from taping the "open" trial. During a break, Orlov's lawyer, Evgeny Shalman, was forcibly removed from the courtroom and locked for a time in an office.

On the trial's last day, I argued vehemently that the defendant's friends should be allowed into the courtroom to hear the verdict. As I made my way through

---

64. *A Chronicle of Current Events*, Amnesty International Publications, Numbers 37, 38, 39, pp. 90-1.

the crowd, a scuffle broke out; first I, then others, were dragged off to police cars parked nearby. I hit one KGB agent; Lusia, receiving a sharp and professional blow to the neck from another one, smacked him back. As she was being shoved into a police car, she accidentally punched the local chief of police. We were released promptly, but were later summoned to appear in court, where we were fined (fifty rubles for me, forty for Lusia) for "hooliganism" – creating a disturbance during a trial. Reluctant to charge us with assault and battery, they ignored Lusia's "I was right to hit the KGB agent, and don't regret it, but I struck the police chief by mistake, and I'd like to apologize to him." The policemen crowding the courtroom no doubt appreciated that remark.

I felt embarrassed when two persons who had been detained with us were sentenced to fifteen days in jail while we got off with a fine.[65]

On 30 October 1976, Sakharov provided written answers to questions from a journalist on Soviet legality:

Q: The Soviet regime says that the dissenters Sergei Kovalev and Andrei Tverdokhlebov were convicted because they violated Soviet law. Can you tell us something about Soviet legality?

Sakharov: What the Soviet legal system, as a whole, lacks is the tradition of impartiality, judicial independence, and the pursuit of justice as an abstract concept. This is apparent not only in its treatment of dissenters. I receive hundreds of desperate letters from people convicted in common criminal (not political) cases and from their relatives. Even allowing for the partiality and prejudice of my correspondents, I still cannot help but be filled with horror at the picture they describe. It is one of judicial tyranny and corruption, of cruelty and the absence of any willingness of those in authority to right wrongs or injustices. Without bothering to collect real evidence, investigators (either themselves or with the

---

65. *Memoirs*, pp. 483-4.

help of other prisoners) often beat the required confession out of the accused. I read about such occurrences in almost every letter I receive. In Kazakhstan, a nineteen-year-old boy, Igor Brusnikin, died this way. Fortunately, we do not hear of such behaviour now in political cases.

Some courts consider even the most serious cases, such as premeditated murder, which carries a death penalty, in a superficial manner, ignoring all contradictory evidence and defence requests. The case of Rafkat Shaimukhamedov, a Tatar worker who was executed by firing squad in January 1976, after two years on death row, is a frightening example of the way our judicial apparatus sometimes works mercilessly and unjustly.

Let's say a political case comes before this kind of court – a case in which the sentence has already been decided at high levels of the KGB. The members of the court know very well that any "independent thinking" will only harm their careers. KGB agents in plain clothes zealously guard the courtroom itself against any unapproved observers of this judicial farce. Can you expect a fair verdict under these conditions?

Kovalev and Tverdokhlebov, as many before them, were convicted under Articles 70 and 190[1] of the RSFSR Criminal Code respectively. The concepts contained in these laws – anti-Soviet agitation and propaganda, slanderous fabrications, the presence of an intent to subvert or weaken the Soviet state and social system – have never been juridically defined. The falsity of the statements or publications which are cited to incriminate the accused cannot be proved by the courts simply because such documents talk about the very human rights violations which are so common in our country. As a result, we get pure demagoguery – you see it confirmed in articles in the Soviet press reporting that Kovalev and Tverdokhlebov were convicted not for their beliefs, but for "specific criminal acts of slander".

Proving the existence of intent to subvert the Soviet system is equally difficult. The goals of the non-violent struggle for human rights, for free discussion and justice, for the openness of Soviet society, are not subversive, but constructive; not political, but humane and civic. All mankind has a stake in the realization of these goals.[66]

Sakharov persisted in his efforts to uphold the rule of law during the first Congress of People's Deputies in 1989:

In the course of the last year a number of laws and decrees have been adopted that are causing great public concern. We don't really know who drafts these laws or how the legislative process works in general. Many lawyers have stated in writing that they don't understand at what stage and in what agencies laws are given their final form.

The 1988 decrees on demonstrations and on the duties and rights of the special forces when engaged in preserving public order are, in my opinion, a step backward in the democratization of our country and contradict the international obligations assumed by our state. They reflect a fear of the people, a fear of free democratic activity, and they have already led to skirmishes in Minsk, in the Crimean village of Lenino, in Krasnoyarsk, in Kuropaty and many other places, and to the tragic explosion in Tbilisi, which has been discussed here. I would like to know what role comrade Lukyanov played in drafting these decrees, whether he approved them, and his personal opinion of the decrees. That's my first question.

My second question concerns the decree of the Presidium of the Supreme Soviet of April 8 [on state crimes]. In my opinion, it also contradicts democratic principles. A very important idea was incorporated in the 1948 Universal Declaration of Human Rights and promoted by organizations such as Amnesty International: acts of conscience that do not involve violence or calls for violence ought not to become the subject of criminal prosecution. This principle is a keystone of a democratic legal system. But the element of "violence" has been omitted from the April 8 decree's definition of criminal

---

66. *Alarm and Hope*, pp. 37-39.

subversion. That is why I find it unsatisfactory. And that decree also contains the notorious Article 11¹ [defamation of the Soviet system]. Unfortunately, the decree has already been applied, individuals have been tried under it, and the Plenum of the Supreme Court has issued a commentary on it (which strikes me as incomplete and unsatisfactory). It's unfortunate when a law or a decree requires external clarification, when it permits differing interpretations. ...

I've received many letters from individuals who feel they have been unjustly convicted and from relatives of convicts. They state that they've appealed to the Procuracy, submitting documents proving that the verdicts in their cases were unjust. Some of the arguments seem convincing. In all instances, the Procuracy sent a stock reply: "There is no basis for reopening the case" without any concrete analysis of the petitioner's arguments. It has been reported in the press that most often the Procuracy doesn't even request the case files for review. I received the same sort of superficial reply to my complaint concerning the conviction of my wife, Elena Bonner. What's your attitude toward this?[67]

Abolition of the death penalty

Sakharov's grandfather, Ivan Sakharov, was a successful lawyer of liberal views. He edited a collection of essays, published in 1906, advocating the abolition of capital punishment. Sakharov read the essays as a young boy and they made a great impression on him.[68]

In 1962, Sakharov wrote to the editor of the weekly *Nedelya* about a case reported in the paper, and asked the editor to forward his letter to the procurator's office. The case concerned an old man in a small town who had counterfeited a few coins and hidden them in his yard. The old man seemed to have used one to buy some milk, and had also hinted about his buried treasure to friends.

---

67. *Moscow and Beyond*, pp. 127-9.
68. *Memoirs*, p. 6.

> Word spread, the old man's house was searched and the counterfeit rubles, wrapped in a handkerchief, were dug up in the garden. The man was arrested, a show trial was held, and he was sentenced to death as a dangerous criminal. The verdict was meant to serve as a deterrent to other would-be counterfeiters; the newspaper claimed it had been handed down in response to "numerous demands from working people."
>
> The punishment struck me as completely out of proportion to the gravity of the crime, if you can really call it a crime at all.[69]

In autumn 1972, Sakharov drafted and gathered over 50 signatures on an appeal to the Supreme Soviet calling for the abolition of the death penalty:

> Many people have long sought the abolition of the death penalty, believing that it contradicts moral sensibility and cannot be justified by any social considerations. The death penalty has now been abolished in many countries.
>
> On the anniversary of the formation of the Union of Soviet Socialist Republics, we call on the USSR Supreme Soviet to adopt a law abolishing the death penalty in our country.
>
> Such a decision would promote the extension of this humane act throughout the world.[70]

At the invitation of Amnesty International, Sakharov wrote the following statement setting out the reasons for his opposition to the death penalty for a Conference on the Abolition of the Death Penalty, held in Stockholm in December 1977:

I regard the death penalty as a savage, immoral institution which undermines the ethical and legal foundations of a society. The state, in the person of its functionaries (who, like all people, are prone to superficial judgments and may be swayed by prejudice or selfish motives), assumes the right to the most terrible and irreversible act – the taking of human life. Such a state cannot expect an improvement in its moral atmosphere. I reject the notion that the

---

69. Ibid., p. 239.
70. *A Chronicle of Human Rights in the USSR*, no. 5-6, 1974, p. 54.

death penalty has any real deterrent effect whatsoever on potential criminals. I am convinced that the contrary is true – that savagery begets only savagery.

I deny that the death penalty is in practice necessary or effective as a means of defending society. The temporary isolation of offenders which may be necessary in some cases must be achieved by more humane and more flexible measures which can be rectified in the event of judicial error and adjusted to take account of changes in society or in the personality of the offender.

I am convinced that society as a whole and each of its members individually, not just the person who comes before the court, bears responsibility for the occurrence of a crime. No simple solutions exist for reducing or eliminating crime, and in any event, the death penalty provides no answer. Only a gradual evolution of society, a growth of humanitarian attitudes which lead people to a deep respect for life and human reason and a greater concern for the difficulties and problems of their neighbours, can reduce crime or eliminate it. Such a society is still no more than a dream. Only by setting an example of humane conduct today can we instil the hope that it may someday be achieved.

I believe that the principle involved in the total abolition of the death penalty justifies disregarding those objections which are based on particular or exceptional cases.

While still a child, I read with horror the remarkable collection of essays Against the Death Penalty published in Russia with the participation of my grandfather Ivan Sakharov in 1906-1907 during the wave of executions following the 1905 revolution. I have read the impassioned statements of Tolstoy, Dostoevsky, Hugo, Korolenko, Rozanov, Andreyev, and many others. From the above-mentioned collection I know the arguments of a number of scholars: Soloviev, Bazhenov (the psychology of condemned persons), Gernet, Goldovsky, Davydov, and others. I share their conviction that the psychological horror associated with the death penalty renders it disproportionate to the vast majority of crimes and inappropriate as a just retribution or punishment in every case. And indeed, how can one speak of the punishment of a person *who has ceased to exist? I share their conviction that the death penalty lacks any moral or practical justification and represents a survival of barbaric customs of revenge – cold-blooded and calculated revenge, with no personal danger for the executioners, with no passionate personal involvement on the part of the judge, and therefore shameful and disgusting.*

I must comment briefly on the widely discussed subject of terrorism. I am of the opinion that the death penalty is completely ineffective in the struggle against terrorism and other political crimes committed by fanatics. In such cases the death penalty serves only as a catalyst for the psychosis of lawlessness, revenge, and savagery. I do not in any way sanction the current phenomenon of political terrorism, which is often accompanied by the death of random persons, by the taking of hostages (including children), and by other dreadful crimes. I am convinced, however, that imprisonment (possibly reinforced by the adoption of a law forbidding release before completion of sentence in cases specified by the court) is a more rational measure for the physical and psychological isolation of terrorists and for the prevention of further acts of terror.

The abolition of the death penalty is especially important in a country like ours with its unrestricted state power, its uncontrolled bureaucracy, and its widespread contempt for law and moral values. You know of the mass executions of innocent people which were carried out during the 1930s and 1940s in a mockery of justice, not to mention the still greater numbers who perished without any legal proceedings at all. We are still living in the moral climate created during that era.

I wish to stress the fact that in the USSR the death penalty is a possible punishment for many crimes which have no relation to crimes threatening human life. You may recall, for example, the case of Rokotov and Faibishenko, who were charged in 1960 with underground traffic in gems and illegal currency operations. After they had been sentenced to imprisonment, the Presidium of the Supreme Soviet passed a law which extended application of the death penalty to large-scale crimes against property. Rokotov and Faibishenko were retried and sentenced to death in violation of the fundamental legal principle barring retroactive application of criminal sanctions. Many other persons have since been executed under analogous laws, essentially for carrying on private business activities. In 1962 an old man was shot for counterfeiting a few coins which he had buried in his yard.

The total number of executions in the USSR is not known; the statistics are a state secret. But there are grounds to believe that several hundred persons are executed annually, a greater number than in most countries where this barbaric institution persists. Other aspects of our life must be taken into account in any discussion of capital punishment in the USSR: the backward and dismal condition of our criminal justice system, its subservience to the state machine, the prevalence of bribery and corruption, and the frequent interventions of local big shots in judicial procedures.

I receive a great many letters from persons convicted of crimes. I cannot check the facts in every case, but taken all together, these letters create an irrefutable and terrible picture of lawlessness and injustice, of superficial and prejudiced investigation, of the impossibility of obtaining review of clearly mistaken or dubious verdicts, of beatings during police questioning.

Some of these cases involve death sentences. Here is one such case. I have before me a copy of the court verdict in the case of Raftat Shaimukhamedov, documents on his case prepared by lawyers, and letters by his mother. On May 31, 1974, in Issyk-Kule, Shaimukhamedov, a worker and by nationality a Tatar, was sentenced to be shot. He had been convicted of murdering a female shop assistant – while intending to commit robbery along with two accomplices. (The latter were sentenced to several years' imprisonment.) Shaimukhamedov denied his guilt, refused to ask for pardon, and declared a hunger strike. He passed twenty months in the death cell expecting either execution or a review of his case. Throughout this time his mother and lawyers submitted dozens of complaints, but all higher authorities sent them back without any examination of the matter. In January 1976 the sentence was carried out with the sanction of Deputy Procurator General of the USSR Malyarov.

The court verdict on Shaimukhamedov is striking for its illiteracy, in both the literal and the juridical sense of the word, given its lack of proofs and its contradictory nature. An even more vivid picture emerges from the complaints of the lawyers and the mother's letters. The convicted person's presence at the scene of the crime was not proved. The court ignored the contradictory versions of the accusation, the testimony of witnesses, and the facts of the expert examination (according to which the victim's blood group did not match that of a spot of blood found on Shaimukhamedov's clothing). The mother's letters state that the reason for this bias lay in the selfish material interest of two procurators (Bekboev and Kleishin). She describes scenes of extortion, bribes received by them from another accused, the fabrication of a criminal case against her second son with the same goal of extortion even after the shooting of Rafkat. I cannot verify these reports, but to me the main message is clear: with what ease and absence of argument the death penalty was passed, and how easily so terrible a case becomes routine.

I have dwelt on this case in detail because it seems to me that it clearly reflects the complete horror of the death penalty and its destructive effect on society.

I hope that this symposium will make a contribution to the noble efforts of many generations toward the complete abolition of the death penalty throughout the world.

19 September 1977[71]

---

71. Translated by Khronika Press.

Protection of the environment

Sakharov attributed what he considered a catastrophic environmental situation in part to immunity from punishment enjoyed by those in positions of power. He writes of interventions at the first Congress of People's Deputies in June 1989:

Other speeches recounted the disastrous ecological conditions in Uzbekistan, the near-extinction of peoples of the North, the radioactive contamination of an enormous region as a consequence of the Chernobyl reactor accident, the pollution of air and water by the chemical and metallurgical industries. The environmental situation of our country is catastrophic and can be attributed in large measure to the pursuit of selfish interests by our gigantic super monopolies and their immunity from punishment, the cause of many of our other difficulties as well.[72]

Lake Baikal

In 1967, I became involved in the effort to save Lake Baikal. For several years, Literaturnaya gazeta and other newspapers had been publishing alarming – and convincing – reports on threats to Baikal from industrial production along its shores, the felling and rafting of timber, and the discharge of chemical wastes into its waters. Though our efforts to protect Baikal were unsuccessful, I did gain valuable insight into environmental problems, both in general and in the particular context of Soviet society.

Early in 1967, a student at the Moscow Institute of Energy visited me on behalf of the Komsomol's Committee to Save Baikal. He invited me to attend the Committee's meetings, to study the issue, and to join in the defence of Baikal. I took the matter seriously, and a few days later I visited the Komsomol building where the meetings were held.

---

72. *Moscow and Beyond*, p. 125.

I conducted some research on my own, meeting with Professor Rogozin, a specialist in the cellulose industry; I learned that in the late 1950s, the minister in charge of the paper industry had ordered the construction of a large cellulose complex on the shores of Lake Baikal. This facility was designed to produce a particularly durable viscose rayon cord for airplane tires. The aviation industry, however, switched from rayon cord to metallic cord, so that whatever rationale the Baikal complex may once have had – and it never, in any case, offset the potential harm to the lake – vanished. Construction nevertheless went ahead, and whole armies of officials, defending their unfortunate decision and their "regimental honour", continued to insist on the importance of the complex for our country's defence, the usual clinching argument.

Building of the complex was already under way when Baikal's defenders discovered that this was the spot where a major earthquake had occurred in the 19th century. Telegrams were duly dispatched to Moscow, but instead of cancelling the project, the authorities transferred responsibility to the Ministry of Medium Machine building, which, as a reward, was permitted to cut timber in the Baikal preserve! ...

The big problem now was the treatment of toxic waste. The appropriate institutes worked out a scheme for biological purification, after which the effluents were to bypass Baikal. The scientists defending the lake pointed to flaws in the proposal, and their fears proved justified when the complex began operating. The Academy of Sciences appointed a commission of experts chaired by a chemist with little competence in this particular field but responsive to the Academy's President and the State Planning Commission.

Our Committee had assembled extensive documentation on the damage to the lake and its surroundings which could come about through human activity. We proposed that the lake shores be closed to new industry and that existing enterprises be moved. Our report was sent to the Central Committee together with a sampling of the seven thousand letters received by Literaturnaya gazeta *and* Komsomolskaya pravda.

For good measure, I decided to telephone Brezhnev personally; it was the last conversation we ever had. He was friendly and courteous, but complained of overwork and suggested that I talk to Kosygin, who was handling the Baikal matter. Unfortunately, I failed to follow up. I had never dealt with Kosygin, did not know him personally, and feared that without preliminary spadework, a call would be useless. My call to the head of state, I thought, was all that was needed. I was wrong.

I soon learned that a final decision had been made at a meeting of the Council of Ministers attended by Mstislav Keldysh, President of the Academy of Sciences. Kosygin asked Keldysh: "What does the Academy recommend? If the safeguards aren't reliable, we'll stop construction." Keldysh reported the commission's conclusion: the water purification system and the other safeguards for Baikal were completely reliable. My feeling is that his stand was greatly influenced by the Academy's administrative dependence on the bureaucratic machine headed by the Central Committee, the State Planning Committee, and the ministries. Keldysh and the Academy's presidium were predisposed to respect the wishes of this machine and to ignore the warnings of whistleblowers, dismissing their arguments a priori *as demagogic, exaggerated, impractical, and generally nonsensical.*

A couple of years after these events, a Komsomol expedition brought back photographs showing the massive destruction of Baikal's fish and plankton caused by toxic wastes. But in accordance with standing instructions, no accidental discharges had been logged. As always, everything was fine on paper.[73]

General Meeting of the Soviet Academy of Sciences

At the General Meeting of the Academy of Sciences on 28 December 1988, Sakharov raised several matters concerning protection of the environment. He urged the academy to call for a halt to the construction of the Volga-Chograi

---

73. *Memoirs*, pp. 277-80.

canal on grounds of cost and concern that diverting water from the Volga River might require rerouting the flow of Russia's northern rivers and also threaten the survival of the osetra sturgeon. He addressed nuclear energy safety, the solution for which, in his view, was to site nuclear power plants underground, and to adopt a worldwide law banning above-ground nuclear reactors since the consequences of nuclear accidents do not stop at national borders. The problems of safety were not, he said, only technological and economic, but also social and psychological, and people could not be held hostage to the endless uncertainty that had increased many times over since the Chernobyl accident in 1986. He called for all information about Chernobyl to be published, and for resistance to its disclosure by agencies that bore responsibility for it to be overcome. He also called for wide-ranging research to identify the extent of damage to humankind's genetic fund caused by exposure to chemicals and radiation. Although research was conducted into the effects of individual chemicals to establish ceilings for their concentration in the air, in lakes, rivers, and drinking water, this was done in isolation from the bigger picture:

> It is necessary to assess the problem in its totality and to understand its consequences for our generation and the generations to come, because genetic defects are accumulating in the mechanism governing heredity. And this is not just about chemicals but about radiation as well. We need to study the extent of the danger created by the disruption of the genetic fund of the human species. You have already heard about the increasing prevalence of mental diseases, which is undoubtedly linked to harmful genetic mutations. It is necessary to develop practical recommendations on this issue. We need to eliminate now from use in our agriculture and elsewhere all strong triggers of genetic mutations. But it may be even more important to exclude weaker triggers of genetic mutation that are being used in large quantities. I believe that safeguarding the world's genetic fund is exceptionally important.[74]

---

74. Remarks on Environmental Issues at the General Meeting of the Soviet Academy of Sciences, published in *Vestnik AN SSSR* 5, 116, 1989.

International responsibility for human rights

When the world's nations adopted the United Nations Charter in 1945, they reaffirmed faith in human rights and made the promotion of human rights and fundamental freedoms one of the three central purposes of the United Nations, pledging to act for their universal respect and observance. The way in which a state treated its own citizens ceased to be exclusively its own affair and became a legitimate concern and responsibility for other states and citizens everywhere. Sakharov never doubted that human rights were a matter of universal concern and responsibility and that they were inextricably linked with world peace and economic and social progress. In an appeal he sent to US President Gerald Ford and Jimmy Carter on 11 October 1976 in advance of US elections in November, he wrote:

> I am convinced that guaranteed political and civil rights for people the world over are also guarantees of international security, economic and social progress, and environmental protection. Freedom of belief and conscience, free exchange of information, freedom of movement, and freedom to choose one's country of residence – such rights cannot be set apart from the basic problems facing mankind. And in defence of human rights there can be no place for isolationism or national self-seeking.

> By broadening the recognition of these principles, the Helsinki declaration has opened new possibilities for international action. Among them is the campaign for a general worldwide amnesty for political prisoners.[75]

Sakharov wrote again to President Carter on 21 January 1977, shortly after his inauguration, asking for his help to secure the release of prisoners of conscience, and providing names of prisoners in the Soviet Union.

> It is very important to defend those who suffer because of their non-violent struggle for an open society, for justice, for other people whose rights are violated. It is our duty and yours to fight for them. I think that a lot depends on this struggle – trust between peoples, confidence in lofty promises, and, in the final analysis, international security.

---

75. *Alarm and Hope*, p. 44.

Carter responded in a letter of 5 February. Human rights, he wrote, were a central concern of his administration, the United States would use its good offices to seek the release of prisoners of conscience and would continue its efforts to shape a world responsive to human aspirations by which nations of differing cultures and histories can live side by side in peace and justice. Encouraged by this response, Sakharov responded the same day.

> Several times I have written and said that the defence of fundamental human rights is not interference in the internal affairs of other countries, but rather one of the most important international concerns, inseparable from the basic problems of peace and progress. Today, having received your letter – and I fully understand its exceptional nature – I can only repeat this once again.[76]

This exchange engendered considerable controversy in the USSR and in the USA where it sparked a major debate on US foreign policy. Sakharov gave the following responses to questions from an American Broadcasting Company correspondent on 25 March 1977:

Q: Since Carter became President, some dissidents have been arrested and you have been threatened with criminal prosecution yourself. Some say that President Carter's position on human rights has led the Soviet government to put stronger pressure on the dissidents. Do you agree?

Sakharov: Categorically – no! Repressions are our daily life. They existed under Nixon, under Ford, and both before and after Helsinki. The latest wave of repressions began during the first days of January – that is, before Carter took office. Of course, by having made public statements on human rights, Carter did assume a certain responsibility.

But if specific actions do not follow general statements, if the public in America and in Europe – legislatures, business people, scientific and cultural organisations in charge of contacts, and labour unions – do not

---

76. Ibid., p. 51.

support these statements and the principles expressed in them, then not only will these people in prison not be freed, but a further intensification of repression may occur.

Q: Many Soviet commentators say that Carter's letter to you is interference in the internal affairs of the USSR. Do you agree?

Sakharov: A personal letter – in which the USSR is not even mentioned— can in no way be interference in its internal affairs.[77]

On 2 May 1981, President Ronald Reagan sent the following message to Sakharov on the occasion of his 60th birthday.

> *I am pleased to add my congratulations to Academician Andrei Sakharov on the occasion of this 60th birthday. Sakharov is one of the true spiritual heroes of our time. An outstanding scientist whose position ensured him all the security and comfort he might desire, he was willing to risk all to speak out on behalf of human rights and freedom. He persisted in this mission even after being subjected to extremely harsh penalties.*
>
> *Mr. Sakharov is a Russian patriot in the best sense of the word because he perceives his peoples' greatness to lie not in militarism and conquest abroad but in building a free and lawful society at home. His principled declarations on behalf of freedom and peace reinforce our belief in these ideals. We hope and pray that his exile will be ended and that he will enjoy a long and creative life on behalf of science and humanity.*

---

77. Ibid., pp. 53-4.

IV. In tribute

Sergei Kovalev

Sergei Kovalev was born in 1930. He enrolled in the Faculty of Physiology at Moscow State University in 1951, and received his doctoral degree in 1959. In his *Memoirs*, Sakharov wrote: "When I met Kovalev in 1970, he'd already published more than 60 papers on neural networks and other topics in neurophysiology on the borderline between biology and information science. In the 1960s he was one of the founders of the human rights movement and helped develop its principles: non-violence, *glasnost*, respect for law, a conscientious attitude toward information. In 1969, after signing protest letters and becoming a founding member of the Initiative Group for Human Rights, Kovalev had been forced out of a senior research position at Moscow University. We didn't see each other all that often, but he became a true friend, close to us in credo and spirit."

Found guilty of anti-Soviet propaganda in December 1975, Kovalev was sentenced to seven years in a labour camp and three years' exile. Denied permission to reside in Moscow after his release in 1984, he worked as a nightwatchman in Kalinin until 1987 when he was permitted to rejoin his wife in their Moscow apartment. In July 1987, he co-founded Press Club Glasnost, which debated and publicised unorthodox views. Following his election to the Supreme Soviet of the Russian Federation in 1990, he was elected chairman of its Human Rights Committee, and appointed to the Constitutional Commission of the Russian Supreme Soviet. He was largely responsible for drafting and securing the passage of the 48 articles of Section Two (The Rights and Liberties of Man and of the Citizen) of the Constitution of the Russian Federation currently in force. He was elected to the new Russian Duma in December 1993, which elected him Russia's first Human Rights Commissioner (ombudsman). An outspoken critic of Russia's December 1994 military attack on Chechnya, though not an advocate of Chechen independence, he considered the bombing of Grozny and Russia's general conduct of the Chechen war a gross violation of human rights. His courageous reporting from Grozny during the war's first month won the sympathy of world public opinion and of much of the Russian intelligentsia for the Chechens' plight. It also alienated President Yeltsin and most Duma deputies, resulting in his dismissal as ombudsman in March 1995 and his resignation from the Human Rights Commission. Kovalev is president of the Human Rights Institute and chair of the Andrei Sakharov Centre in Moscow.[78]

The following excerpts are from an article Kovalev wrote in 1998.

Andrei Dmitrievich Sakharov: Meeting the demands of reason

Sakharov was my close friend. ...

Sakharov played an enormous role in my life: with his opinions, his advice, and his constant participation in my fate not only when I was in jail, but also later, in Moscow, when he returned from his Gorky exile in 1986, two years after my return from exile in Magadan.

I have tried to write about Sakharov dispassionately, as if about a man I did not know. The only liberty that I take is to call Sakharov by our nickname for him: A.D. [the initials of his first name and patronymic]. ...

* * *

I am not a physicist, and therefore I will not risk talking about the scientific genius of Sakharov. Instead, I will discuss those aspects of Sakharov's civic activity which are relevant for our time and for humanity's future.

---

78. In compiling this biographical note, extensive use was made of Emma Gilligan's *Defending Human Rights in Russia: Sergei Kovalev, Dissident and Human Rights Commissioner*, Routledge Curzon, London, 2004.

But doesn't everybody know everything about his deeds already? "Sakharov was leader of the human rights activists in the USSR, an indisputable moral authority for dissidents throughout the Soviet Union." This characterization of Sakharov's role in the civic life of our country has become almost a commonplace in our time. And there is a great deal of truth in it. ...

Sakharov never claimed to be "anti-Soviet," even though, like the rest of us, he did not approve of many practices and policies of the Soviet regime. But his thought and action moved in a completely different realm. For a long time, he nurtured the hope that the Soviet government would be capable of reforming itself (experience showed that he was right) and that in doing so, it would not collapse, but would rather be strengthened (experience showed that here he was wrong). This did not have a decisive significance for A.D. – he was primarily concerned about a divided world and how to overcome this division? Getting used to Sakharov's global thinking was difficult, and for many – impossible.

Sakharov was an adviser. For a long time, he was close to our leaders and was accustomed to talking with them. He did not renounce this custom even after he was openly declared the government's Enemy No 1. He stubbornly continued to give advice to those who stood at the helm, and it was not his fault, but the country's loss that they did not listen to him. This applies not only to Sakharov, but to most of the prominent human rights advocates of the 1960s and 1970s. We didn't fight against the Soviet government and didn't intend to do so. It was another matter that the Soviet government fought against us with all its might – but that says more about the government's reflexes than about our intentions.

During the perestroika *years, few of Sakharov's like-minded colleagues condemned his practice of "accommodation". The majority of dissidents understood and accepted his position ... A.D. was not a saint, and not even a preacher of holiness. I think he believed that to change social reality requires, above all, constructive decisions. And each of his appeals, beginning with his first public statements in the latter half of the 1960s, always contained constructive proposals. It is another matter that these proposals were incompatible with the hidebound thinking of Soviet true-believers, and later, of dogmatic democrats. ...*

Returning to the subject of Sakharov's civic position, Sakharov's human rights activity was inseparable from his political views, and this sharply distinguished him from other human rights advocates in the USSR. He was in no way a politician in the traditional understanding of this word, since he understood that traditional politics was a dangerous anachronism. It was not that he occupied some position between pure politics and pure human rights. It was a synthesis of two different approaches to civic issues that had seemed distinct. The struggle for human rights in the framework of this new world view would take on a particular depth and significance, because it would become simultaneously a struggle for the future of humankind. Political activism would also be transformed, since the criteria for evaluating it would change: political abstractions, like "national interests", would give way to guaranteeing the rights and interests of each member of the human community. ...

It seems to me that the particularities of Sakharov's approach were closely connected with his scientific thinking. One of the outstanding achievements of Sakharov the scientist was to investigate the relevance of quantum mechanics – the laws of physics in the micro-world – to cosmology's explanation of the origin of the Universe. One result of this approach, and a currently accepted hypothesis, was Sakharov's paper "Violation of CP Invariance, C Asymmetry, and Baryon Asymmetry of the Universe" which Sakharov published in 1967. In 1968, Sakharov published Reflections *relating freedom of the quantum of society – the individual – to the development of humanity – our social universe. Didn't Sakharov's thinking about cosmology give rise to his idea of multiple options for society's development, which is similar to the idea that the laws governing the micro-world are probability-based? I will say more, whatever physicists may think of the idea: the endless and seemingly fruitless efforts of A.D. to defend specific people, time after time, appeal after appeal, reiterating calls for the release of prisoners of conscience – Vladimir Bukovsky, Vladimir Osipov, Anatoly Shcharansky, Sergei Kovalev, Paruir Airikyan, Anatoly Marchenko and dozens and dozens of others – appeals which unfailingly concluded Sakharov's articles and speeches, no matter the topic – did these only ensue from a natural moral sense? Didn't he anticipate that these small sparks might initiate a chain reaction leading to the self-liberation of society? If so, then the experience of 1987-1989 would prove the correctness of his vision.*

The term "chain reaction" forces us to think about the main paradox, perhaps, of Sakharov's biography. In fact, for the majority of people, Sakharov, the physicist, is not so much the author of the theory of baryon asymmetry of the Universe, induced gravity or managed thermonuclear synthesis – he is "the father of the Soviet hydrogen bomb," the most terrible weapon ever invented. How may we reconcile this fact with A.D.'s later civic activity?

About four years ago, the writer Viktor Astafiev accused Sakharov of hypocrisy: "Having created a weapon that could incinerate the planet, he has never repented. Such a subterfuge – to die a hero, having committed a crime."[79]

The late Ales Adamovich, who regarded Sakharov with enormous respect, believed just the opposite: that Sakharov's civic activity in fact was his repentance. Adamovich was perplexed, however, when Sakharov himself categorically denied this hypothesis. I think that Adamovich did not believe this denial; he thought that Sakharov simply did not like people prying into his soul.

I believe that Astafiev was more correct than Adamovich.

Of course, any creator of a weapon of mass destruction had to experience some emotion. We know this firsthand from the designers of the American atomic bomb, Robert Oppenheimer and Leo Szilard, and also from the theoreticians

---

79. *Izvestiya*, 30 April 1994.

Einstein and Bohr. And Sakharov is no exception. In his Memoirs, *we find only a few sentences on this topic, and no repentance. On the contrary, in several places, Sakharov writes directly that he continued to believe his work in creating the hydrogen bomb was correct and useful. And he explains why.*

This is what is interesting about his explanations: there is not a word of patriotism, which would have motivated the participation in the project for nine out of ten people in his place. Sakharov speaks about something else: the significance of this work for all of humankind. Is this a paradox? Not so. It was simply that A.D., to the end of his life, believed that if a super weapon were to become the monopoly of a single country, the situation would be fraught with enormous danger. And in this premise, correct or not, there was only scientific analysis, free from ideological or national prejudice and without a trace of anti-Americanism or xenophobia. (In 1948, Sakharov still harboured certain illusions regarding the Soviet system, but by the mid 1960s, he was rid of them; he nevertheless continued to work at Arzamas-16 until he was barred from defence work.) I don't think that he feared an unprovoked U.S. nuclear attack but he supposed that in the absence of nuclear equilibrium, the danger of the outbreak of a "conventional" war would be many times greater, and it would inevitably escalate to a Third World War. That means he viewed his work on the hydrogen bomb as a means of preventing a global catastrophe.[80] *...*

From the tangled knot of problems, Sakharov picked out the most severe and urgent one: the danger to human life of the radioactivity resulting from the testing of nuclear weapons (this was a comparatively new problem, and Soviet physicists knew little about it). Sakharov was horrified by his estimate of the number of victims caused by such tests. A.D.'s statement in 1961 against ending a previously-declared moratorium on testing became his first "civic" action. I place this word in quotes, because Sakharov's protest was entirely behind closed doors and expressed itself in insistent, but private demands to

---

80. I recall Albert Einstein's response to the question about what kind of weapon would be used in the Third World War: "In the Third, I don't know, but in the Fourth – sticks and stones."

government officials. It angered Khrushchev, who was outraged at this blunt interference by a scientist in political matters. But Khrushchev's complaints did not stop Sakharov, just as the more severe measures taken against him by Brezhnev and Andropov did not stop him. And he did achieve his goal: it was his proposal that formed the basis for the Moscow Treaty of 1963 [prohibiting above-ground and underwater tests].

Later, Sakharov repeatedly spoke out on nuclear disarmament. Each time his opinion was balanced, reasonable, and proceeded not from abstract ideological or moral dogma, but from existing realities. It was constructive – that is the main difference between Sakharov's political initiatives and the statements of most pacifists.

* * *

The Sakharov approach to the nuclear threat beautifully illustrates the particularities of his thinking: constructive proposals, a sense of scale, and complete intellectual freedom. ...

Some say that Andrei Dmitrievich Sakharov was a herald of the "new thinking". Others called him "the founder of a new morality". It's nothing like that!

A.D. was the bearer of an absolutely normal way of thinking as old as the world – that is, thinking based on reason. His intellectual activity, whether it concerned science or politics or human rights, completely corresponded to the qualities that define a real scientist. These qualities of the intellect can be summarized in three words: fearless, selfless, and passionless.

A new morality? Not at all – it is the most ordinary human morality, only consistent. The last time it was formulated with such extreme clarity was about 2,000 years ago, and I do not think that A.D. added anything new to that formulation. Yet again, it is no accident that in the ancient teachings, the fruits that enable us to distinguish good from evil grow on the tree of knowledge. Ordinary human morality, unlike the holiness of the saints and the righteousness of the prophets, is based on reason and on nothing else. And Sakharov's faithfulness to moral principle is simply another example of the responsibility of a scientist.

The power of Sakharov's intellect is another matter. It accounts for the impression of novelty in Sakharov's thinking and the sense of the uniqueness of his moral strength.

Our tragic century (like the one before it) was beset by the demons of anti-intellectualism and irrationalism. And to be sober and remain sober in a world of drunks, to be awake in a world of sleepers is unusually hard.

Andrei Sakharov was a champion of Reason. It accounts for his democratic convictions and public life. Democracy is the only attempt in history to try to construct a society on a rational foundation.

Some place Sakharov in the same ranks as Mahatma Gandhi, Lev Tolstoy and other prophets of non-violent change. Some are inclined to compare him with Alexander Solzhenitsyn and Lech Walesa – outstanding fighters against tyranny. These associations have their rationale. Personally, I prefer to compare the physicist Sakharov to the geochemist Vladimir Vernadsky, who proposed the concept of the Noosphere – our Earth as it has been shaped by human reason – and to the biologist Teilhard de Chardin, author of the "anti-entropy" theory of evolution, and other initiators of a new holistic philosophy of knowledge, in which the development of humanity is turned into a factor of cosmic significance.

I believe that Andrei Sakharov would find such a comparison interesting.

Sergei Kovalev, 1998 [81]

---

81. *Izvestiya*, 21 May 1998. Translated by Fitzpatrick, C. A. for the Andrei Sakharov Foundation (USA). © Sergei Kovalev, 2010.

Valentin Turchin

(14 February 1931 – 7 April 2010)

Valentin Turchin graduated from Moscow University as a theoretical physicist. He worked on the theory of nuclear reactors and neutron scattering from 1953 to 1964. From 1965 to 1972 he worked at the Institute of Applied Mathematics of the Academy of Sciences specialising in information theory and computer science. He became head of a laboratory at the Institute for the Design of Automated Construction Systems in 1973, but was expelled from the Institute in 1974. In 1968, his essay *The Inertia of Fear*, was widely circulated in *samizdat*. He also hosted an informal seminar, which examined ideological, philosophical, and historical questions in the aftermath of the Prague Spring. In September 1973, he signed an open letter in defence of Sakharov when Sakharov came under fierce attack following the interview with Olle Stenholm. After the arrests of Kovalev in December 1974 and Tverdokhlebov in April 1975, and numerous protests by Turchin on their and others' behalf, he came under increasing pressure. Blacklisted, unable to find work, and repeatedly harassed by the KGB, in July 1977 Turchin wrote to Brezhnev reiterating an earlier request to move to the United States temporarily to work as a computer scientist. He was allowed to emigrate in October 1977, thanks in part to interventions by scientists in the USA, and began work as a research scientist at New York University's Courant Institute of Mathematical Sciences in January 1978. He visited Russia in 1990, where he conducted an international seminar in Obninsk, a centre for atomic science 60 miles from Moscow.

My memory of Andrei Dmitrievich Sakharov

Not long before my departure from Russia, a remark appeared in an American newspaper, or maybe a journal, to the effect that Sakharov, after all, is only a general without an army. An American correspondent in Moscow asked me what I thought about it. Is it true? Of course not, I said – but not because Sakharov has an army, but because he is not a general. Outstanding public figures who leave their imprint on history may be divided into two categories: leaders and saints. The leaders show other people what they can (although they, maybe, should not) do. Thus they are followed by masses. The saints show others what they should (although they, maybe, cannot) do. Thus, they are followed, if at all, by a handful of dissidents.

Sakharov is from the category of saints. I had the privilege of closely knowing Andrei Dmitrievich. His is a personality which makes everyone better who comes in touch with him. His human kindness, his non-compromising, absolute honesty has been a shining beacon for all of us. When you speak with Sakharov you keep wondering at his amazing simplicity, his absolute artlessness. To understand Sakharov, it is essential to remember that he is a scientist, a scientist to the marrow of his bones. He started his life as a scientist par excellence; Sakharov the public figure is the result of the evolution of Sakharov the scientist. Essentially, he took the high standards and values of science, first of all that of truth, and applied them to problems of social life and politics. It was not easy, and it required tremendous courage. The crowd of his former colleagues betrayed and ostracized him.

I remember an episode. It was in September 1973, soon after the infamous letter of forty academicians condemning Sakharov. I was sitting with the Sakharovs – in their kitchen, as usual – and discussing the letter. The Sakharovs had just returned from a Black Sea resort, and Lusia (Elena) told me about a funny occurrence which took place a couple of days before they left. They were taking sunbathing at the beach, when a short man ran up to Andrei Dmitrievich, showed him how glad he was to meet him, shook his hand, and several times repeated how fortunate it is that such a person is among them. "'Who was that?" asked Lusia when the short man departed. Andrei Dmitrievich answered that it was an academician so-and-so. Three days later, when the letter of forty[82] was published, that academician was among the signers.

---

82. *Pravda* published a letter on 29 August 1973 signed by 40 members of the Academy of Sciences, alleging, *inter alia*, that "Sakharov has made himself an instrument of propaganda hostile to the Soviet Union" and "his actions discredit the good name of Soviet science."

Lusia, who is generally emotional, spoke with contempt and indignation, which were certainly well justified. I looked at Andrei Dmitrievich: what is his reaction? It was very typical for him. Sakharov was half-smiling and pensive. He showed no contempt. He was not indignant about the episode. He was thinking about it.

Though Sakharov's name is universally known, the full impact of his personality on the developments on the world's scene is still to be appreciated in the future. We know from history that when new civilizations emerge, it is the saints and prophets who come first; leaders come later. Humanity is in desperate need of a new and more sound basis for the goals and values of the new global civilization that is now in the throes of birth. I see Andrei Sakharov as a prophet of this coming civilization. He demonstrates that the heights of moral strength, courage, and self-sacrifice are not necessarily based on any of the traditional religions which now separate the human race. Nor do they require a belief in the supernatural or in life after death. They may take root in the sober and critical but compassionate human thinking so characteristic of Andrei Dmitrievich.

Valentin Turchin, 1985 [83]

Valery Chalidze

Valery Chalidze was born in 1938 in Moscow. His mother, an architect and city planner, was responsible for his upbringing after his father, an engineer, was killed at the front in 1942. Chalidze studied physics at Moscow and Tbilisi Universities. Until 1970, he headed a research unit investigating the physical properties of polymers at Moscow's Plastics Research Institute. From 1969 to 1972 he published a *samizdat* journal *Social Problems*, which focused on human rights issues. He was the moving force in founding, with Tverdokhlebov and Sakharov, the Moscow Human Rights Committee in November 1970. In

---

83. *Andrei Sakharov and Peace – an Anthology*, Avon Books, 1985, pp. 319-20.

November 1972, Chalidze was permitted to visit the United States, together with his wife Vera, but on 13 December, Soviet Embassy officials came to his New York hotel, confiscated his passport and informed him that he had been deprived of his Soviet citizenship for actions discrediting the state. In 1973 in New York, Chalidze founded and directed Khronika Press, a major publisher of human rights materials from the USSR, including works by Sakharov, and issues 28-64 of *A Chronicle of Current events*. Random House published English translations of two books written by Chalidze, *To Defend these Rights* (1975) and *Criminal Russia* (1977).

Andrei Sakharov and the Russian intelligentsia

We must look to the early nineteenth century in order to understand the origins of the Russian intelligentsia. Until then culture in Russia was closely associated with the court and depended on the patronage of the crown. During the reign of Alexander I – perhaps as a by-product of his unrealized liberal tendencies – some creative talents abandoned the court and, while not yet forming a separate social caste, gathered in intellectual circles which were independent of the state power, and even inclined to oppose it.

The rupture was not abrupt. The poet Alexander Pushkin, known for his love of liberty and for his independence, recognized before his death that the alienation of educated society from authority and from the official state hierarchy was strange and unnatural. Pushkin was partly ready for reconciliation with the Emperor. But the divorce of culture from the Russian state proceeded although not everyone recognized the process while it was occurring.

Why have I begun with such ancient history? Because we cannot understand Sakharov's role in Russia today unless we know the epic of the intelligentsia. Sakharov is a heroic figure, and admired everywhere for his appeals on behalf of human rights and fundamental freedoms. But he is also a tragic actor in the drama of Russian history and of the Russian intelligentsia.

Who is guilty in the conflict between state and intelligentsia in Russia? Both parties, I believe. The authorities because they want to subordinate culture to their own purposes and turn the intelligentsia into propagandists for imperial greatness. The intelligentsia, because in warring against the state for two centuries, they turned their backs on normal politics and have played an exclusively negative role, first as critics of the prevailing order and then as destroyers of that order. The Russian intelligentsia constitute a unique social group. I have not discovered any western counterpart. Intellectuals do exist in the West, and they may oppose the government, but they do not form a separate, coherent caste.

The intelligentsia fostered the fall of the Russian Empire, but after the Revolution, the intelligentsia remained in opposition and the new regime made war upon the social group which had created it. The very nature and beliefs of the intelligentsia seem to require opposition to the government in power. We have learned much about the bloody persecutions of the intelligentsia during the Soviet era, but we know too that its traditions survived and continue to enrich world culture. But the tragedy for the Russian nation is that the intelligentsia have excluded themselves from practical politics. The intelligentsia as a matter of principle refuse to participate in the decision-making process of the state. Moreover, the intelligentsia scorn the common man's striving for a career and success. I remember my own friends in Russia – they thought the word "career" somehow disgusting. Their ideal is a selfless dedication to culture, to the ideals of art and science with almost no regard for recognition by society.

From one perspective, Sakharov's way of thinking, his ethical principles, even his opinions are typical of the Russian intelligentsia. On the other hand, he not only served in official posts; he rose high in the state hierarchy and did much to make strong the existing regime. It is well known that Sakharov made notable contributions to the military applications of thermonuclear reactions. For many years he occupied a leading post in the military-industrial complex, and he received the highest State awards for his accomplishments. Similar cases were known earlier. Intellectuals had served successfully in official posts, but as a rule they no longer were considered intelligentsia in the Russian sense.

But Sakharov never stopped being an intelligent. *His faculty for independent thought about society as well as about science never atrophied, although social criticism is a taboo subject for private Soviet citizens. Sakharov made no effort to camouflage his opinions. After working inside the establishment for many years, in 1968 he published his outspoken views on the course of Soviet society and on the dangers threatening the world. His essay* Progress, Coexistence and Intellectual Freedom *was a sincere attempt to initiate a dialogue to which the regime could well have responded. His act was, however, too unexpected, and the state hierarchy expelled Sakharov. The regime once more displayed the symmetry of its relations with the intelligentsia. The intelligentsia totally reject the regime, and the regime replies in kind. Of course, the symmetry is not complete, because the authorities send the intellectuals to prison and exile.*

Sakharov's public activity has turned him into a symbol of liberty, of opposition to tyranny. He has said many wise and good things. But I believe that he will be remembered in future history books as one of those rare intellectuals who dared to break down the wall between power and culture, disregarding the moral taboos of his social group and the lack of understanding of the authorities.

Earlier attempts to build bridges between state and society foundered because they were out of phase. Alexander II introduced important reforms which should have been welcomed by the intelligentsia, but they disdained gradual progress. In the second half of the nineteenth century, they began sharpening the axe which cut off many heads of the intelligentsia after 1917.

History is ironic. The intelligentsia might have gone to meet Alexander II's reforms or Nicholas II's creation of a parliament. But the moments were lost and instead the current dissident movement had to begin by seeking a dialogue with Mr. Brezhnev. By then the authorities were deaf and blind. They rejected the intelligentsia's attempt, and so the country remains at war with itself.

Forecasts are risky, but I believe it possible and desirable that in the future the situation in Russia will lead the regime to undertake co-operation with the intelligentsia without insisting that they abandon their principles or tell lies. And perhaps circumstances will change sufficiently so that in Russia as in other civilized countries the intelligentsia will no longer consider participation in the political process shameful and will be willing to assist in the government of their country. This may sound utopian, but Sakharov's example shows that it is possible. He worked within the government establishment and still remained an honest man and a member of the Russian intelligentsia.

Sakharov's tragedy is not his interrupted career, not the lack of success of many of his human rights initiatives, not even his current exile in Gorky. His tragedy lies in his attempt to overcome the two-hundred-year antagonism between the intelligentsia representing the culture of society, and the authorities representing the power of society.

No single cause can explain the tragic course of Russian history for the last two centuries, but the hostility, the lack of mutual understanding between the state and the intelligentsia was surely a significant factor. Elimination of this conflict is absolutely necessary for Russia's health in the future. The ice must be broken by brave individuals. Sakharov was the first and most prominent man of our age who – while holding important state posts – remained a member of the intelligentsia and openly expressed their beliefs.

Valery Chalidze, 1981[84]

---

84. This speech was delivered at the American Physical Society's Special Symposium to Honour Andrei D. Sakharov, New York, 26 January 1981, and published in *Russia*, No. 2, pp. 5-6. © Valery Chalidze, 1981.

Pavel Litvinov

Pavel Litvinov was born in 1940 in Moscow. He graduated from Moscow University in 1964, and taught physics at the Institute for Chemical Technology until he lost his job in 1967, as a result of his activities in defence of human rights which intensified after the arrest of his friend, Alexander Ginzburg, in 1967. Litvinov became a prominent voice in the emerging human rights movement in the USSR. In October 1968, he was exiled to Siberia for five years for organising the 25 August 1968 demonstration in Red Square to protest the Soviet Union's invasion of Czechoslovakia. He continued to speak out after his return to Moscow in November 1972 which led to his emigration to the United States in 1974, where he taught physics at the Hackley School in Tarrytown, New York, until retiring in 2007.

Litvinov was editor of *The Demonstration in Pushkin Square* (Harvill Press, 1969) and *The Trial of the Four* (Viking 1972). He was a member of the Russian-American Project Group on Human Rights from 1989 to 1996, and has been Chairman of the Society of Friends of Memorial since 1992. In December 2008, he received the "Hasten To Do Good" medal awarded by Vladimir Lukin, Human Rights Commissioner of the Russian Federation. Litvinov's 8 August 1968 letter to Stephen Spender asking him to help "support and defend those in the USSR undergoing persecution for civic or literary activity and provide information to world public opinion about the real state of affairs in the USSR" is credited with being indirectly responsible for the establishment of the journal *Index on Censorship* and the organisation Writers and Scholars. Litvinov contributed this tribute to Sakharov for a conference organised at Harvard University in October 2008 "40 Years after Andrei Sakharov's Reflections on Progress, Peaceful Co-existence and Intellectual Freedom: Russia Yesterday, Today and Tomorrow."

In search of dialogue

First of all, nobody should mention me as a physicist together with Andrei Sakharov because my physics achievements are more than modest. I haven't done much physics since I was expelled from graduate school and lost my job as an assistant professor of physics, and that was in Moscow in 1968. Since that time, I have only been a teacher of physics.

My life intersected with the life of Andrei Sakharov before we met in person. I was one of the early activists among those who became known as "Soviet dissidents," although we didn't call ourselves that. That name came later. We preferred to call ourselves "human rights advocates". In 1965 we started a movement to defend human rights as they were reflected in the Soviet Constitution and the Universal Declaration of Human Rights. We wrote letters protesting violations of human rights, we wrote about the fate of political prisoners, about Soviet censorship, about confining people in mental hospitals for their political convictions. The movement grew, and the first half of 1968 could be considered one of its high points. By that time, I had already lost my position as assistant professor of physics and I was involved in many samizdat *publications. With help, I edited several books. But the most important thing I was doing was meeting regularly with foreign correspondents in Moscow and giving them* samizdat *materials, mostly letters of protest. There were hundreds of people signing letters of protest after the arrests of people like Sinyavsky and Daniel in 1965; Ginzburg, Galanskov, and Bukovsky in 1967; and many others. Protests and arrests were continuing.*

Everybody should understand that at that time, the only means to copy samizdat *materials for circulation was a simple instrument called "the typewriter". It was before personal computers were available; Xerox-type copy machines barely existed and they were kept under state control in the Soviet Union. The only way a person could express his views on Soviet issues, other than speaking with friends in "kitchen conversations," was to type something on a manual typewriter – electric typewriters didn't exist – using carbon paper to make multiple copies. Most of you, depending on age, have probably used or heard of carbon paper, but as a teacher, I have already met young people who have never seen a typewriter in their lives. The KGB – the*

Soviet security police – and the authorities generally in the Soviet Union weren't interested in serious public discussions unless they were officially organized and published in Soviet newspapers and journals. Censorship of everything printed in the Soviet Union was total at the time. There were periodicals such as the journal Novy Mir *and the newspaper* Literaturnaya gazeta *where occasional discussions were permitted, but they were officially controlled discussions. During the 1960s,* samizdat *– the distribution of manuscripts in typewritten form – was born.*

I was one of the early and very active dissident leaders. I and my friend the late Andrei Amalrik were the "press officers" of the human rights movement, as Amalrik jokingly called us. We would meet foreign correspondents regularly and give them samizdat, *which would be smuggled out of the country, printed in the* New York Times, Le Monde, *or other publications, and then broadcast by Western radio stations like Radio Liberty, Voice of America and the BBC back to the Soviet Union, so that many Soviet citizens who couldn't be reached directly by* samizdat *would hear about its content.*

In 1968, another friend of mine, a physicist from the city of Obninsk whose name was Valery Pavlinchuk, brought me a manuscript. It was signed by Andrei Sakharov, and it was called Reflections on Progress, Peaceful Co-existence and Intellectual Freedom. *I had heard of Sakharov, but almost no one knew his name, because he was a super-secret scientist who lived in a super-secret city where weapons research was conducted. Even in an officially published Academy of Sciences reference book, he was mentioned simply as "Andrei Sakharov, member of the Academy of Sciences,* otdeleniye tekhnicheskiky nauk *(section of technical sciences). Nothing about his achievements or who he was. Physicists talked about him among themselves and discussed his very few published scientific papers. I remember I heard about his paper on the theory of a magnetic thermonuclear reactor or "Tokamak," when I was in Moscow University; and there were a couple more of his papers which I didn't read at the time.*

His work on thermonuclear weapons was secret. But one thing we knew: that Sakharov spoke up at meetings of the Academy of Sciences against the worst political hacks whom Soviet officials tried to promote in the Academy of Sciences, people like Nuzhdin and Trapeznikov. That was practically all we knew. And suddenly, I received Sakharov's essay from my friend from Obninsk. As I learned later, he had been given this paper by Zhores Medvedev, the biologist, who was then a friend of Sakharov, as was his twin brother Roy Medvedev, a historian. Pavlinchuk said Sakharov wanted me to have his essay. I asked, "What do you mean, to have it?" And he said, "Well, he just wanted you to read it." "Does he mean that I should send it abroad? Does he want it to be published and circulated in samizdat*?" I asked, and Pavlinchuk answered, "Yes, yes, of course." That was the end of our conversation.*

I read Sakharov's essay that evening, and then brought it to Amalrik. We were completely amazed by this article; it was extremely interesting for us, but not primarily because of its content. For me, for Amalrik, and for many others of our circle, this article seemed a bit mild. At that time, we went much farther in our criticism of the Soviet regime, and we were much more radical in our attitude towards Communism. I don't like the word "anti-Communist," but we completely rejected the Soviet regime, and most of our friends were dissidents. Some of our friends, like Pyotr Yakir and General Grigorenko, still used a kind of official Soviet language in their petitions and in their writing for samizdat, *but they were rapidly getting over this habit.*

What amazed us was that this essay was written and signed by Sakharov – a great scientist, a person who was from the establishment and who was close to the country's leaders. That was incredible. Another important factor for many people, surprisingly, was that Sakharov wasn't Jewish, that he was an ethnic Russian. He was publicly expressing his ideas about intellectual freedom, about the threat of the destruction of humankind, about the danger of nuclear war, about the need for cooperation between nations, and he put both superpowers – the Soviet Union and the United States – on the same level. He was definitely a person who came to these ideas from his own serious thinking. I felt that I had to do something – Sakharov's essay had to be distributed.

Every Saturday, Andrei Amalrik and I met our friend, Karel von het Reve, who would receive samizdat from us. He was a correspondent in Moscow for the Dutch newspaper Het Parool. He was an absolutely brave man, much braver than the average foreign correspondent in Moscow. He received Reflections from me, looked at it, and he too was amazed. He took it to his apartment in Moscow and immediately translated it into Dutch. He read his translation over the phone to his newspaper in Amsterdam, trusting that any censor listening in would not understand the Dutch language. That's why the first publication of the essay was in Het Parool on July 6, 1968. Karel gave the essay to Ray Anderson, a young, inexperienced, but also intelligent and honorable correspondent of The New York Times, who took it for advice to Henry Shapiro, a senior correspondent of United Press International. Shapiro, a veteran Moscow correspondent but an extremely cautious man, said, "It can't be. There's no such man as Sakharov. It was Litvinov who wrote it. Better not touch it." Nevertheless, after some delay, Ray Anderson sent it to the United States, where it was published in full in the New York Times on July 22. Sakharov's essay became a world sensation. In 1968-69 more than eighteen million copies of it were published around the world in more than a dozen languages.

Today we can see that Sakharov's ideas evolved after he wrote Reflections. After he was barred from work on weapons and the authorities wouldn't listen to him, he became a dissident, and one of the best and bravest human rights defenders. During all the years he spent defending human rights and criticizing the Soviet regime, he never forgot about his idea of peace. If you reread Reflections, you will see that his ideas about economics, about nuclear war, about nuclear power, about tolerance, about human rights live on. Sakharov was a great man of peace. I am just amazed at how great a contribution Sakharov made to his country and the world.

Pavel Litvinov, 2008

Yuri Orlov

Yuri Orlov was born in 1924 in Moscow. Orlov served as an officer in the Soviet army from 1944 to 1946, graduated from Moscow State University in 1952, and then worked as a physicist at Moscow's Institute of Theoretical and Experimental Physics. He was expelled from the Communist Party and fired from his job for a pro-democracy speech he made in 1956. He found work at the Yerevan Institute of Physics, where he was elected a corresponding member of the Armenian Academy of Sciences. In 1972, Orlov returned to Moscow and worked at the Institute of Terrestrial Magnetism. He was fired in 1973 after becoming a founding member of the first Amnesty International group in the USSR. In May 1976, he organised and became chairman of the Moscow Helsinki Group. He was arrested in 1977 and sent to labour camp in 1978. He was released in October 1986 and deported to the United States.

Currently Professor of Physics and Government at Cornell University, Orlov has consulted at Brookhaven National Laboratory and is the author of *Dangerous Thoughts: Memoirs of a Russian Life* (William Morrow, 1991). These are excerpts from Orlov's tribute to Sakharov at the October 2008 Harvard Conference "40 Years after Andrei Sakharov's Reflections on Progress, Peaceful Co-existence and Intellectual Freedom: Russia Yesterday, Today and Tomorrow".

I believe I first met Sakharov about 1967. I first met Sakharov's wife Elena in 1973 when I visited her and Sakharov in the Academy of Sciences hospital where she was being treated for a thyroid condition and he was having his heart tested. ...

First, let's remember what was happening in the early 1950s. Stalin was still alive. According to the official press, medical doctors tried to poison Stalin. It was not true, but the doctors were put in prison. There were also campaigns against "cosmopolitans," geneticists, and others. There was an attempt to condemn Einstein's theory of relativity and Bohr's quantum theory as pseudo-scientific concepts, but that campaign was stopped on orders from above.

The question – "What were the political ideas of scientists in the late Stalin era?" – makes no sense at all if we recall that probably 15 percent of scientists were forced by the KGB to write denunciations. In my group of students at Moscow University's Physical-Technical Department, at least 25 percent of them were denouncing each other. Some of them came to me later and described what was going on. In such a situation, to ask about their political views is a silly question.

The situation changed rather quickly after Khrushchev's speech to the Twentieth Party Congress in 1956 denouncing Stalin. I was a young scientist then at the Institute of Theoretical and Experimental Physics (ITEP), and a member of its Party Committee. After Khrushchev's speech, I was asked to help organize a meeting of the Institute's Communists to discuss the situation. We, the Party Committee, prepared for it well, rehearsing who would say what.

I was more of a theoretician. Although I was a Marxist, I didn't believe in determinism. In my speech, I said that the socialist economic system was all right, but the political system can be repressive or terrorist. I used the phrases "terror policy" and "socialist but not democratic country." I suggested the Soviet Union should become more liberal like Yugoslavia. I also talked about the moral degradation of the Soviet people from the top to the bottom.

Another member of the committee, Vadim Nesterov, talked about freedom of information and asked why the Soviet Union was jamming the BBC.

All our speeches are available now. Drawn from the Party archives, they have been printed in various publications. I was very happy to read my own speech; I had forgotten large parts of it.

Those were our very radical thoughts as young scientists. I wasn't familiar with human rights concepts at that time. What I had were revolutionary thoughts: arming the workers and resisting a future bureaucratic regime. Earlier, in the mid-1940s when I was an officer in the Red Army, my personal view was that we didn't have a dictatorship of the working class; we had a dictatorship of the bureaucracy.

What was the reaction of leading scientists to our speeches? All the Communists of the entire Institute lost their Communist Party cards because they supported us during that meeting. They had to condemn in writing our speeches and apologize for not having condemned them at the meeting. Those who did not write properly did not get their Party cards back. And a week later, we, the organizers, lost our jobs.

The director of ITEP, Abram Alikhanov, summoned us to his office. He explained that he had called Khrushchev on our behalf, and Khrushchev said, "I'm not alone in the Politburo. All I could do was see to it that they weren't arrested." When Alikhanov asked him not to fire us from the Institute, Khrushchev said that was impossible. Alikhanov concluded our meeting by saying, "If you knew what you were doing, you're heroes. If you didn't, you're fools."

That was the 1950s. During the 1960s, most scientists were quiet. Probably one reason was that in the early part of that decade, there was a movement among them to join the Communist Party "in order to transform it from inside," as some of them explained to me. I was rather sceptical at the time, saying that the Party might transform them instead of being itself transformed. Now I think that this movement wasn't bad for the time.

The 1960s was of course the period when dissidents emerged in force. And 1968 was a peak year: in April there was the first issue of the samizdat journal A Chronicle of Current Events; in July Sakharov's Reflections; in August the demonstration on Red Square by Pavel Litvinov, Bogoraz, and six others protesting the Soviet invasion of Czechoslovakia. On May 20, 1969, the Initiative Group for the Defence of Human Rights, founded by Pyotr Yakir, Viktor Krasin, with fifteen members, including Sergei Kovalev, issued an appeal to the United Nations on behalf of Soviet political prisoners. (There was no response from the United Nations at that time.)

I had decided to concentrate on physics and eventually became a Professor and a Corresponding Member of the Armenian Academy of Sciences. However,

Sakharov's essay, first, and the demonstration on Red Square, second, made me ashamed that I had done nothing after 1956 to promote democracy and human rights. So 1968 was a turning point for me. But I didn't want to do something insignificant. If I simply opened my mouth in Yerevan, the next day I would find myself on the way to the Urals.

In 1973, I became a founding member of the first Amnesty International group in the Soviet Union. In May 1976, I organized the Moscow Helsinki Group and served as its chairman until my arrest in February 1977.

As I have said, Sakharov's essay and the demonstration on Red Square were crucial for me in 1968. As for the reactions of scientists generally to Reflections, *Pavel Litvinov in his talk has described them completely correctly. It was not important* what *was written in the Sakharov article. It was important that Sakharov* wrote it. It was his position both in science and in the political structure of the Soviet Union that made it important. *Reflections* completely contradicted the official line. To say that we needed democratization was a crime, because we were supposedly the most democratic country in the world.

There were quite a few scientists like Gersh Budker, who in private conversation with me or in my presence expressed serious concern about the fate of Sakharov and discussed how to help him if he were to be punished.

In the 1960s, scientists in the Soviet Union were generally supportive of critics of the regime. But most scientists, particularly in the provinces, did not sympathize with sending criticism abroad. They considered involving foreigners anti-patriotic.

Yuri Orlov, 2008

Interview with President Mikhail Gorbachev

This interview with President Gorbachev was conducted by journalists Yuri Rost and Dmitri Medvedev in November 2004. It was first published in a special edition of the journal *Novaya Gazeta* in May 2005.

Gorbachev: Let me tell you a story. Once, while working as Party boss in Stavropol, I got a call from Moscow, just when I was about to leave for my yearly vacation. The call was from the Ideological Department of the Party's Central Committee. They told me: "You have Academician Pyotr Kapitsa vacationing nearby in Kislovodsk. Talk to him, if you can. Find out whether he could help influence Sakharov to bring him back into the mainstream."

All right, I was going to talk to Kapitsa, though academicians are not easy to deal with. This would be an interesting meeting, and a pleasure for me. I decided to do it, but also thought to myself: why was I being steered in this direction? But that's how things were getting done back then. So we met. We sat down, had some tea, and talked. He came with his wife.

Kapitsa was the real thing, a true Academician. I broached the topic of Sakharov rather cautiously. Kapitsa replied: "Andrei Dmitrievich made a gigantic contribution to defense research. He was awarded the Order of Hero of Socialist Labour three times!" This was no news for me. But I also knew that he had become a subject of negative writings, and that the higher-ups had no idea what to do about him. They reasoned that, even though he had indeed provided them with the bomb and resolved their most important task at the time, still, he had received awards from them, and thus he owed them, not vice versa. That was their mindset, while their underlying concern was that Sakharov was unmanageable. That's why I was asked to talk to Kapitsa, to find out whether he could influence Sakharov. But Pyotr Leonidovich responded as follows: "Academicians are exceptional people. But even among them, Sakharov is special. That's why he's constantly concerned about the political order in the country. What did he do wrong? He had written letters to the Central Committee, which was the right address. He's disciplined. He mailed his reflections to them. But Mikhail Suslov, the ideological leader of the Party, didn't like it. So Sakharov got a call from a low-level official – a desk officer, not even a department chief. There was neither real discussion nor substantive response. He felt disrespected. So he went and published his reflections abroad. That set the ball rolling."

To tell the truth, Sakharov was a loyal citizen. And his reasoning about peaceful co-existence, convergence and democracy was correct. The ideas that essentially foreshadowed *perestroika*.

Rost: How did you come up with the idea of bringing Sakharov back to Moscow from his internment in Gorky?

Gorbachev: I was constantly aware of the problem of Sakharov's deportation. He was in Gorky when I became General Secretary. This was a difficult time, and initially other problems seemed more important, as they, indeed, were. This caused a delay in thinking about how to bring him back. And I had no idea that among the country's leadership I would be supported on this issue by Yakovlev, Shevardnadze, and Vadim Medvedev, while everyone else would be against it.

Finally, I said: "OK, please give me Sakharov's file. He was deported to Gorky, so there must be a file with a paper trail of decisions." After all, I am a lawyer. To make a long story short, the Sakharov file did not reach my desk. It simply didn't exist. There was nothing except the resolution or the decree that ordered him to be sent away from Moscow.

Rost: How come there was no Sakharov file? That's impossible.

Gorbachev: There was no case file that could serve as a basis for the legal decision. There was nothing but rumours and reports: here is what he said to X and what he told Y; he gave an interview to this one and to that one. So, I said: "If that's the case, let's discuss Sakharov at our next Politburo session."

There was not much of a discussion. For it was clear to all that he was wrongly punished: he did not contravene the Constitution which endorsed freedom of speech. Besides, all the points he made were weighty and well-grounded.

As a result, we had to come up with a procedure: how do we bring him back to Moscow? There was a suggestion to send Alexandrov, the president of the Academy of Sciences, on a mission to Sakharov. But I had a gut feeling that it was not quite right, given that he was deported by a decision of the Politburo, as far as I can remember. Finally, I said: "Let's do it this way: I will talk to him myself." So, they got a phone installed in his apartment. When I was told that the line was working, I gave him a call:

"Hello, Andrei Dmitrievich. This is Gorbachev." – "Hello, how are you?" – "I want to tell you that you can go back to Moscow, return to your apartment and do your work. Everything that you had remains in your possession, so get back to work, in the Academy and elsewhere." He didn't thank me. And he was right – there was nothing to thank me for. He immediately started telling me: "All the prisoners of conscience must be set free," etc. etc. Nothing about himself. He also told me about Anatoly Marchenko who was in dire condition … I replied: "Andrei Dmitrievich, go back to Moscow, that's what I wanted to tell you, and then we'll look into all these issues."

I told my colleagues about this conversation and said: "Please submit your proposals on political prisoners."

Overall, getting to know him was a boon for me. Particularly at the moments when I had to make drastic decisions to move to a new level of democratic transformation. And I was able to rely on him because his judgments were always thoroughly substantiated. His arguments bore his stamp, but they were logical and free of bitterness. He both stirred controversy and set the tone of debate for the entire country. And he was very active, never sitting on the fence. He came forward with his own draft constitution. He spoke up, he advocated the transfer of power to the Congress of People's Deputies, on the basis of it having been elected by the people.

Rost: Were Sakharov's pronouncements helpful to you?

Gorbachev: Absolutely.

Rost: Even those things that you didn't agree with?

Gorbachev: Absolutely... all of it was very important. I'm sure he knew it. Now, looking at your interview with him, I see how even more valuable it was.

Rost: So, he understood what was going on here, and so did you?

Gorbachev: Right.

Rost: This means that you were engaged in some kind of an implicit dialogue?

Gorbachev: No question about it. After all, I was giving him the floor at the Congress even though I sensed the irritation of those who were sitting on the dais. But it was important to let him speak.

Rost: I remember once I was driving with him in the car after a session and I told him: "Elena and I were worried about you. Gorbachev kept interrupting your speech." And Sakharov replied: "Gorbachev had the power not to let me speak at all. But he was letting me speak. I had a feeling that he wanted me to speak: he couldn't say what I could, but he needed the words to be spoken."

Gorbachev: The mass of people needed a push to turn them toward democracy. But it was a complex task. Sakharov was aware of it.

Rost: Did you possess leverage yourself, as General Secretary?

Gorbachev: If I didn't, there would have been no Congress.

Rost: But you couldn't say what Sakharov could.

Gorbachev: You're right. I couldn't. How could I? The entire Congress would have gone crazy. Just read its transcripts. What a thriller! I sometimes read them. They're so striking. We needed to move forward, but without losing our heads. It was the first time that these individuals found themselves in the position of freely elected representatives of their people. For the first time in their lives, they were going through a school of freedom – freedom of speech, of public debate, of disagreement, of real struggle.

Rost: Had you anticipated the magnitude of the risks involved? Were you fully aware of what you were getting into?

Gorbachev: Of course I was. After all, what was *perestroika*? An immense risk. Had I been in my seventies, a tempered, tired man, I most likely wouldn't have gotten into it.

Rost: Was your verbosity a conscious attempt to disguise your actual goals? Sakharov believed that you were in a difficult position, having to manœuvre all the time between the old Politburo and new ideas.

Gorbachev: Well, I couldn't allow the Congress to break into a fight and fall apart.

Rost: That's not my point. I think you had only a few like-minded supporters in the Politburo, a minority.

Gorbachev: You can think what you want. You're a free man. But let me make another point. Here is a telling story about Andrei Dmitrievich that shows him in action outside the confines of the Congress. Once after the end of a session, somewhere between 7 and 8 pm, I was sitting down with my assistants, with Georgy Shakhnazarov – who was then actively involved in high politics – and many others whom I prefer not to name here. Every evening I worked late hours. Upon finishing my work, I was leaving my office that was adjacent to the Congress hall. The lights in the hall were off. I said to my aides, "We're done for today". They tell me: "But you have someone waiting for you." "Who's that?" "Sakharov." "Why didn't you tell me earlier?" "He told us that he would wait until you were finished."

I stepped out into the hall. He was sitting in the corner on the stage, on a chair next to the curtain. They put him there, gave him a cup of tea or something, and there he was, sitting. I said to him: "Andrei Dmitrievich, good evening! Are you staying here overnight?"

"No, I just need to see you. I have a very serious matter to discuss." "Okay, fine." I took a chair and sat next to him. So, we were sitting next to each other, facing the hall – an empty, vast, dark congress hall.

I asked: "So, how do you like the Congress?" He replied – and I sensed how he was talking to me: just the same way as to you or anybody else – without softening his remarks. Someone who has a strong opinion and sticks to it may emphasize this or that, may develop his thought in this or that direction, bring up new arguments – but the hard core is always there.

Sakharov said to me: "You see for yourself what kind of a Congress this is – it's very conservative." "Yes it is, but just think of it, Andrei

Dmitrievich, this is our first Congress of this kind, and we have all of it unfolding before the eyes of the entire country, of the entire world! It's hard to imagine what we're into; we still don't quite understand what's going on." "Yes, you're right ..." "So what's your concern?" "You know, I'm afraid that all these conservatives who seem to be dissatisfied with the Congress and how it's going, can force you to backtrack from your positions." Sakharov realized that my policies were the maximum that was feasible at that time and in that context.

Rost: Your policies involved compromises, but compromises in favour of progress.

Gorbachev: I said to him: "If you were you in my place, you'd be thinking about how to control this assembly, about how to manage this great process." "That's not my point. They say the right-wingers have some kind of compromising information about you that they might be able to use it to change the course of our Congress." This was his most important concern.

I replied: "If this is what's worrying you, Andrei Dmitrievich, you can relax and sleep soundly. I have never taken bribes, and I'm sure I won't take any in the future." Of all things, this was never a part of my record. "See you tomorrow," I told him. "We have a lot more work to do." So we parted on good terms.

Rost: It sounds as if he was concerned about your reputation?

Gorbachev: He was concerned that the Congress might change its direction. He realized I was the only one who could prevent that.

He was speaking from the floor a lot, many times more than other Congress speakers. Of course, it was to my advantage to let him speak. He was a responsible person. He was a committed democrat. He was a man of conscience with high ethical standards.

Rost: If Sakharov were still alive, what do you think would be his role and place today?

Gorbachev: He was in the right place during his lifetime. He was a remarkable scientist. He was our moral authority. And for me he was generally an authority. He would be taking the same stands as he took while he was alive. He would be committed to the idea that our country cannot exist in the modern world without further democratization, without the establishment, development and strengthening of social institutions, without safeguarding liberty. He insisted that freedom and democracy are needed to make life worthwhile. And I agree with him.[85]

President Boris Yeltsin

In 1999, President Yeltsin paid this tribute to Andrei Sakharov when he nominated him to be *Time*'s "Person of the Century."

Andrei Sakharov was not a professional politician, but heads of state and the world's leading politicians paid attention to his words. Moved by his conscience and his ethical convictions, academician Sakharov dared to publicly challenge the all-powerful machine of the totalitarian state. He helped many of us take a new look at our own country and at the way we live. I knew him personally and he influenced my views. Sakharov was the real spiritual father of democratic change in Russia. I am intensely aware of how much we miss his wisdom, firmness and humanity today. I am grateful that I had the chance to work alongside Andrei Sakharov.[86]

---

85. Translated by Glinski, D. for the Andrei Sakharov Foundation (USA).
86. *Time*, 20 December 1999, p. 29.

President Dmitry Medvedev

President Medvedev sent the following message on 14 December 2009 to participants in the international conference "Andrei Sakharov's Ideas Today", which was held in Moscow in December 2009 to mark the 20th anniversary of Sakharov's death. It was organised by the Moscow Andrei Sakharov Centre, with the support of the Council of Europe's Commissioner for Human Rights.

Andrei Sakharov, a world renowned scientist and human rights activist, firmly believed that the future is created by all of us, and that it is important to strive for moral self-improvement. He clearly understood that freedom and responsibility are inseparable. His own destiny serves as an example of a life spent following one's conscience and adhering steadily to the principles he defended, fearlessly and selflessly.

Dr. Sakharov feared that alienation was a major threat to humanity and insisted that only equal co-operation, openness and respect for every personality will allow us to preserve and develop our civilization. Today, looking at recent history, we can fully appreciate the depth and relevance of Andrei Sakharov's ideas which are in tune with the challenges faced by modern Russian society.

Efrem Yankelevich

Efrem Yankelevich was born in 1950 in Kharkov. He married Elena Bonner's daughter, Tatiana, in 1970 when studying the technology of radio transmissions at Moscow's Institute of Communications. After the marriage of Sakharov and Bonner in 1972, Efrem became the target of continual KGB harassment. His applications to travel to the United States in 1973 and 1974 were refused, but in September 1977 he emigrated to Newton, Massachusetts, with his wife and their two children. In his *Memoirs*, Sakharov writes: "At our first meeting in July 1971, I recognized my son-in-law's uncompromising fidelity to principle, his integrity, and sure grasp of situations. Following my exile to Gorky,

I made Efrem Yankelevich my official representative abroad, but even earlier, from the moment they arrived in the West, he and Tatiana were forced to take on the burden of representing my ideas and interests; no one else could match their authority. Efrem and Tatiana were constantly having to rush off on business connected with my affairs, to give a talk, or to turn out an article overnight."[87] After his marriage to Tatiana broke up, Efrem moved to Israel, and then returned to Moscow, where he died from a heart attack in 2009. The following excerpts are taken from Efrem Yankelevich's introduction to Andrei Sakharov's *Collected Works*, published in Russian by Vremya, Moscow 2006.

Sakharov's alternatives

Sakharov possessed, in my view, in addition to his other talents, one that was quite rare: the ability to empathize with human suffering and misfortunes no matter where they occurred – whether it was the anonymous victims of nuclear atmospheric testing scattered throughout the world, starving Africans, Soviet prisoners or Palestinian refugees in Sabra and Shatila. (Was this an innate gift or was this capacity developed in him later, when as the "father of the hydrogen bomb" he sensed himself to be responsible for the fate of the world, is a question beyond the framework of this essay).

The "planetary nature" of thought, or rather world view of Sakharov also proceeded from his conviction about the inseparability of the fates of humankind, which he shared with his forerunners Albert Einstein and Niels Bohr. We are all in one boat and we will perish or be saved only together.

And finally, Sakharov believed that social and technical progress can and should relieve human suffering. More precisely, Sakharov supposed, and this was an expression of his democratic convictions, that free people are capable of intelligently building their social life and intelligently using the fruits of scientific progress. ...

---

87. *Memoirs*, pp. 346, 488.

Sakharov's doctrine rests on three arguments. First, if a state represents a threat to its own citizens it will be a threat to its own neighbours. Second, respect for human rights guarantees democratic oversight over a country's foreign policy and over military expenditures, and society will not permit the militarization of the economy during peace time. And Sakharov's third argument was that observance of human rights would guarantee the free exchange of information and ideas between peoples and foster their rapprochement and the lowering of mutual distrust and thus reduce the likelihood of conflict and the possibility of the secret harbouring of aggressive intentions. All of these arguments Sakharov expresses in various contexts in most of his speeches.

* * *

In conclusion, I will speak about what interests me the most, and I suppose the reader as well. What would Sakharov like to see Russia become? If a "Sakharov Party" were to emerge in Russia some day, what would be written on its banners or in its political program?

In Reflections, *Sakharov declared himself a socialist. And although later, his views on the "country of victorious socialism" changed a great deal, and he became an opponent of "totalitarian socialism," I believe that he still remained a socialist or a social-democrat. We do not know for sure what he saw as the flaws of "capitalism", which he nevertheless supposed was "closer to the truly human society" if needed social reforms were adopted than "totalitarian socialism." He did not seem impressed by unbridled capitalism, a society governed solely by the market, by the laws of supply and demand. He may have considered as irrational and wasteful an economy in which economic growth and employment are maintained by artificially stimulating demand. Moreover, Sakharov, as a person of egalitarian views, was, indisputably, close to John Rawls's principle that differentiation in income is justified only to the extent it serves the common good. Sakharov formulates approximately this principle in* Reflections. *Furthermore, he thought that the question of distributing the "social pie" in time would lose its urgency thanks to scientific and technological progress, which would produce material abundance.*

In a word, Sakharov was not a "marketist" of the New Russian sort. Nor was he an American liberal, considering the state a necessary evil. I suppose that Sakharov, to employ the expression of his American friend Edward Kline, saw in the state an instrument for realizing social ideals. And the socialism of Sakharov consisted of seeing in the state not only an instrument for defending rights and liberties but also a provider of social welfare.

It is hard to say precisely what Sakharov had in mind for the "convergence" society. With the exception of social programs and the state sector of the economy, we do not know precisely what traits of socialism Sakharov would preserve. For example, should the planned nature of the state sector of the economy be preserved and how would this be combined with the independence of state enterprises which Sakharov advocated? It is obvious that Sakharov was proposing a socially-oriented economy, an economy designed to achieve social goals not maximum profit, an economy guaranteeing employment and a high level of wages.

Of course, Sakharov understood the danger of leaving to the state too much economic power. I think that he would approve the statement of another socialist, Albert Einstein:

> Nevertheless, it is necessary to remember that a planned economy is not yet socialism. A planned economy as such may be accompanied by the complete enslavement of the individual. The achievement of socialism requires the solution of some extremely difficult socio-political problems: how is it possible, in view of the far-reaching centralization of political and economic power, to prevent bureaucracy from becoming all-powerful and overweening? How can the rights of the individual be protected and therewith a democratic counterweight to the power of bureaucracy be assured?[88]

We know Sakharov's recipes for resolving these problems. It is respect for human rights based on law and an independent judiciary. It is a mixed economy. It is glasnost and oversight of the state sector of the economy and

---

88. Einstein A., *Why Socialism?*

the state bureaucracy by democratic bodies of government (for example, parliamentary committees).

* * *

Sakharov's antidote to the usurpation of power by the federal centre is outlined in his draft Constitution. In his draft, Sakharov transfers to the subjects of his federation (which were then Union Republics) more powers, including its own law-enforcement and judicial systems. The most important point of his program, however, is the financial independence of the subjects of the federation, which, if they were to lose it, would cause them gradually to lose all the rest of their independence. Sakharov proposed that they would make only fixed payments defined by treaty to the federal treasure. All the rest of the subject's revenue could be spent at its own discretion.

Russian intellectuals have long been preoccupied with the search for a "national idea," in fact today, as always, the leading candidate is the idea of "great Russia," or rather "a great state" (at one time autocratic and Orthodox, then socialist, and now, apparently, only anti-Western, with a Russian Orthodox, patriotic colouring). Sakharov in his draft Constitution proposes another national idea, the idea of national altruism in the name of the survival of humanity and the resolution of global problems. ...

In his Constitution, "the global purposes of the survival of humankind" is placed higher than state interests. The purpose of a nation is proclaimed to be "a happy, meaningful life, material and spiritual freedom, well-being, peace and security for the citizens of the world, for all people on Earth regardless of their race, nationality, sex, age or social status."

The idea of national altruism is an idea that is not entirely alien to Russian dissident tradition. Thus, Pyotr Chaadayev wrote: "Russia is too powerful to conduct a national policy; its purpose in the world is a policy on the scale of humanity. Providence created us too great to be egoists; she placed us beyond the interests of nationality and assigned us the interests of humankind."

Therefore, who knows; Sakharov's call for national altruism may be heard some day.

Another important choice facing Russian society, and perhaps, its most important choice, is whether Russia will hew to the forms of social and political organization traditional to it, as the "nationally-minded" pundits propose, or will decisively break with the Tatar-Byzantine political tradition with its vertical model of decision-making, reject its old social ideas and try to adopt new ones. Judging from his polemics with Alexander Solzhenitsyn,[89] Sakharov preferred a break with the past.

I suppose what shocks the outside observer in contemporary Russian society is the absence of any social ideals defining the norms of public life and providing points of departure for socially significant discourse. They have been replaced, as Sakharov wrote, by a cult of the state and power, and now also of money and success. The social ideals which Sakharov put forward are respect for human rights, tolerance and freedom. And if the "Sakharov party" – the Russian citizens who believe in these ideas – succeeds some day in advancing them in public awareness this would be Sakharov's main victory, and also that of Russian society. The future, I hope, will show how Russian society will realize Sakharov's ideals: whether Russians will copy Western institutions or will succeed in inventing and implementing new viable mechanisms.

Efrem Yankelevich, 2006 [90]

---

89. See Sakharov's article "On Alexander Solzhenitsyn's 'A Letter to the Soviet Leaders'" in Maximov, V. (ed.), Fitzpatrick, C. A. (trans.) *Kontinent*, Anchor Books, Garden City NY, 1976, pp. 2-14, note 89.
90. Translated by Fitzpatrick C. for the Andrei Sakharov Foundation (USA).

Václav Havel

Václav Havel was born in Prague in 1936. He is a writer and dramatist and former President of Czechoslovakia and the Czech Republic. After the suppression of the Prague Spring in August 1968, Havel was banned from the theatre. In 1977, he co-founded Charter 77, which called for adherence to the human rights provisions of the Constitution, the 1975 Helsinki Final Act, and the United Nations International Covenants on Human Rights. In April 1978, he was one of the founders of the Committee for the Defence of the Unjustly Prosecuted which was established to assist Charter 77 supporters who had been detained, lost their jobs or suffered other repercussions. Havel and other Charter leaders were tried in October 1979 for subversion. He was imprisoned three times, spending almost five years in prison in all. In November 1989, he became a leader of Civic Forum, a movement demanding fundamental political change in Czechoslovakia. On 29 December 1989, he was elected President of Czechoslovakia and re-elected in free elections the following July. After the dissolution of Czechoslovakia, he served as the first President of the Czech Republic from 1993 to 2003. Havel wrote this preface for Andrei Sakharov's *Collected Works*, published in Russian by Vremya, Moscow 2006.

Preface to the *Collected Works of Andrei Sakharov*

Andrei Sakharov's samizdat *essay* Reflections on Progress, Peaceful Co-existence and Intellectual Freedom *first appeared in Czechoslovakia at the very height of the Prague Spring. It was even published in Czech in the summer of 1968 as a supplement to the* Mladá fronta *newspaper and immediately provoked great interest and comment.*

For Czechoslovakia, which was seeking a peaceful and orderly way of changing the nature of the Soviet regime which had been imposed upon the countries of Eastern Europe following the end of the Second World War, Sakharov's thinking – and at the time we knew very little about who exactly Andrei Dmitrievich Sakharov was – had a special meaning for us. His

Reflections presented themselves not simply as a literary text but as a form of political manifesto. This is what made the text and its author so unusual and appealing.

During the years of Czechoslovakia's "normalisation", which was played out under the conductor's baton of the Soviet occupying forces, we all observed with great interest how this well-known academic and creator of the Soviet hydrogen bomb fought for human rights and civil liberties. Sakharov's statements filled us with hope during the years of occupation.

The awarding of the Nobel Peace prize to Andrei Sakharov in 1975 was seen by Czech dissidents as an award for their efforts too. The announcement of the eminent academic's release from exile in the town of Gorky in December 1986 greatly encouraged the Charter 77 movement. It demonstrated that the Soviet regime's powers were coming to an end and that in a relatively short period of time change could also be expected in the countries of the so-called Soviet bloc.

Unfortunately I never managed to meet Andrei Sakharov in person. He died at the height of Czechoslovakia's "velvet revolution". I learnt from my friends that he had been overjoyed by these developments and had been following them with great interest.

One of my first trips abroad after I was elected President of Czechoslovakia took me to Moscow in February 1990. I took this opportunity to visit Sakharov's grave and pay my respects to this great man. The grave was covered with flowers and wreaths which were brought there every day by hundreds of ordinary people.

I do not wish and furthermore am not qualified to rate Andrei Sakharov as an academic. I am, however, able to rate him highly as a thinker and humanist. There can be no doubt that the influence which Sakharov the Citizen exerted on the world's political development went far beyond the boundaries of his country and his era. His premature death prevented him from fulfilling the tasks he was destined for by virtue of his immense moral authority, his moral purity (something which even Nikita Khrushchev spoke admiringly of), his integrity, courage and originality of thought. Andrei Sakharov was needed by the new Russia of yesterday, he is needed by it today, and he will be missed by it in the future.

The publication of Andrei Sakharov's diaries, memoirs and political essays to mark what would have been his eighty-fifth birthday is a wonderful initiative. This collection of Sakharov's essays will inspire not just us, his contemporaries, but also future generations of citizens who care about the fate and future of our planet.

Václav Havel, Prague, December 2005

Adam Michnik

Adam Michnik was born in Warsaw in 1946. He studied history at Warsaw University. A leader of the student March 1968 protests, he was expelled from the university and sentenced to three years in prison. Released under an amnesty a year and a half later, he worked as a welder for two years, then as private secretary to the poet and columnist, Antoni Slonimski. He completed his history degree at Poznan University in 1975. Following a crackdown on striking workers in 1976, Michnik co-founded the Workers' Defence Committee, known as KOR, to assist imprisoned workers and their families. KOR also supported the underground publication of independent bulletins, periodicals, and books, in which Michnik was involved as editor and essayist. In 1977, KOR was renamed the Committee for Social Self Defence, but retained the same acronym. It was a precursor to the independent trade union, Solidarity, founded in 1980, of which Michnik was an advisor. He was interned in December 1981 when the government imposed martial law, and imprisoned again in 1985. He participated in the 1989 Round Table talks between the Government and Solidarity and in June 1989 was elected to the new parliament. Solidarity's campaign bulletin, *Gazeta Wyborcza* (the *Electoral Gazette*), became the largest daily newspaper in Poland, with Michnik as Editor-in-Chief. Michnik made this tribute to Sakharov on the occasion of the international conference "Andrei Sakharov's Ideas Today" which was held in Moscow in December 2009 to mark the 20th anniversary of Sakharov's death.

Sakharov from a Polish Perspective

Andrei Dmitrievich Sakharov – there was the man and there is the legend. I saw the man only once in my life – on 16 October 1989. That is why I will speak about the legend. Sakharov was a key figure for the democratic movements in the Soviet bloc. He was a scientist, working in a field of supreme importance for the state. Sakharov was highly successful. He was esteemed and rewarded by the government. He could feel secure.

But after observing what was going on in the world, Sakharov chose another path, the path of great Western physicists, like Einstein. He warned the world against nuclear war. In the West such a position required courage and an effort of imagination. In the Soviet Union it required heroism.

Members of the democratic movement have often been called "losers," with unhealthy ambitions and a lust for power. Such thoughts are patently false if applied to Sakharov. He is proof of the rationality of democratic protest.

He began with a belief in reforms and persuasion, in peaceful co-existence and convergence. In the end he advocated comprehensive opposition and unvarnished truth. But he never called for revolution or violence. He remained uncompromising when that was necessary, but ready to compromise when desirable.

His position with respect to violence and revolution was similar to that of Einstein, Martin Luther King, the Dalai Lama, John Paul II, and Vaclav Havel. His position was not that of a politician but rather that of an eyewitness to history who had been drawn into politics.

The most important values for him were freedom and the dignity of the individual. He didn't believe in the wisdom of the crowd, of the masses who can be easily manipulated. He didn't believe in ethnic nationalism or in imperialism. He was a Russian patriot, of the Chekhov and Herzen style. That's why he condemned Soviet intervention in Czechoslovakia in 1968 and in Afghanistan in 1979.

Protest against the wrongful policies of his government was his form of patriotism. When the Soviet Union was at war with Hitler he believed that "Our cause is just" but he no longer believed this to be true in the case of the intervention in Czechoslovakia.

He paid a very high price: he became the victim of a furious slander campaign, of discrimination, and of isolation in Gorky, enforced by constant and oppressive police surveillance. All this took a toll on his health and led to his early death. If one day the democratic world constructs a Pantheon for its saints, Andrei Sakharov will be in that Pantheon.

Sakharov for us was a source of strength and hope, but he was also a challenge. Many of us changed our lives when we saw what he was doing. Unlike the reformers of bolshevism he was not bound by dogma, and he was free from other "isms". For example, he never believed in nationalist-religious mysticism; he was the son of the rationalist and liberal tradition. He was not a fanatic devotee of any doctrine – for him, living people were more important than any abstract doctrine.

Having returned from exile in Gorky he chose the path of compromise and selective support for perestroika, *unlike many emigrants and dissidents. He was not a man who was perpetually dissatisfied or obsessed with revenge. He did not believe "the worse – the better". He understood that "worse is worse", and "better is better". And he did all he could to make it better. He wanted a democratic and normal Russia in a democratic and normal world. His speeches in the Soviet parliament promoted this idea.*

Sakharov was a man of civil society, not a party politician.

He left us this legacy:
a) Patience and fidelity to principle;
b) Pluralism and willingness to compromise – we must accept that honest disagreements will occur;
c) Tolerance;
d) "The better – the better";
e) The patriotism of free peoples: a nation that persecutes another nation cannot itself be free;
f) Fidelity to historic truth;
g) Renunciation of violence.

I conclude with some words of Leszek Kolakowski which, I am convinced, reflect Andrei Sakharov's view: "No victory is irreversible, no defeat is definitive. That is what makes life worth living".

Adam Michnik, December 2009

Thomas Hammarberg

Thomas Hammarberg, Commissioner for Human Rights of the Council of Europe, made this tribute to Sakharov at the international conference "Andrei Sakharov's Ideas Today" which was held in Moscow in December 2009.

The relevance of Andrei Sakharov's example and message on human rights in today's world

Andrei Dmitrievich Sakharov was a unique voice of moral conscience who could not be silenced even by the repressive machine of a super power. His principled messages inspired others and contributed to the non-violent, revolutionary changes of 1989 and thereafter.

Although the world has changed dramatically during the past twenty years, not least in Russia and in Europe, issues which Sakharov confronted continue to be acutely relevant. He was indeed ahead of his time.

Re-reading now his famous essay Reflections on Progress, Peaceful Co-existence and Intellectual Freedom *from 1968 I was struck by the precision of his analysis and importance of his advice on many matters which are topical today, for instance his call for a broad program to eradicate hunger; laws to protect freedom of the media and access to information; measures to encourage truth-telling about the past; and strong measures to prevent environmental degradation.*

Human rights were already in the late sixties a centre piece in his message. He wrote that "[t]he goal of international policy is to ensure fulfilment of the Universal Declaration of Human Rights and to prevent a sharpening of international tensions or a strengthening of militarist or nationalist tendencies."

He defined intellectual freedom *to include freedom to receive and impart information, freedom for open-minded and fearless debate and freedom from authoritarian and prejudiced pressure.*

He saw the repression of these freedoms as a threat to the independence and worth of the human personality, as a threat to the meaning of life itself.

These freedoms are also a condition for real democracy, he stressed: "We need intellectual freedom today to enable the general public and the intelligentsia to assess and control all the actions, projects and decisions of the ruling group."

Typically, he added a pragmatic point about the quality of decisions – errors are inevitable when decisions are reached by secret advisors or shadow cabinets.

The ultimate denial of intellectual freedom was the imprisonment of individuals for merely having expressed their opinions. He had called for the release of political prisoners already in appeals before Reflections.

He continued to stress the importance of fighting political imprisonment through the years. When I served as Secretary General of Amnesty

International in the early eighties he reached us in London from his exile in Gorky with the suggestion about a global campaign for the release of all Prisoners of Conscience. As a result an appeal with more than one million signatures from all over the world was later presented to the President of the General Assembly and the Secretary-General of the United Nations.

Sakharov was alarmed by the inhuman conditions in Soviet prisons and criticised the misuse of psychiatry, the involuntary detention in mental institutions of those who disagreed or disobeyed. He became an unofficial ombudsman for minorities such as the Crimean Tatars, for Baptists and others who suffered religious discrimination and for Jews who wanted to leave the country.

He took a clear position against capital punishment and regretted that he was prevented from coming to the international conference against the death penalty in Stockholm 1977. The message he sent argued for a total abolition:

"I regard the death penalty as a savage, immoral institution which undermines the ethical and legal foundations of society. The state, in the person of its functionaries (who, like all people, are prone to superficial judgments and may be swayed by prejudice or selfish motives), assumes the right to the most terrible and irreversible act – the taking of human life."

"Such a state cannot expect an improvement in its moral atmosphere. I reject the notion that the death penalty has any real deterrent effect whatsoever on potential criminals. I am convinced that the contrary is true – that savagery begets only savagery."

He identified hatred as a major danger for society. He argued persistently for measures against national and racial prejudices and religious intolerance. Particularly unforgivable was state incitement of hatred against "others".

Sakharov's clear and well-argued positions on these crucial human rights issues had an impact – primarily on activists in the Soviet Union, other Communist countries but also in the rest of Europe. Also some governments responded positively. The so-called dissident movement, a movement of moral conscience and resistance, did influence the international discourse on human rights to a considerable degree.

There has certainly been progress on these issues in the past twenty years or more. An understanding has spread that it is shameful and unethical to violate the agreed standards on human rights. Governments do not want to be seen to arrest, try and imprison individuals just because of their views and opinions.

However, at the same time the authorities in some countries have learnt to apply new techniques to silence critics. Also, there are today other repressive forces than the governments themselves, some of them in secret collaboration with the security forces while others are "free-lancing".

- *The number of clear-cut cases of Prisoners of Conscience has gone down considerably but other serious threats have emerged against those who have tried to speak out, including those who work for the defence of human rights.*
- *Human rights activists have been assassinated by contract killers and the culprits have not been seized and brought to justice. This has created a dangerous atmosphere of impunity and fear which discourages civic and human rights activism.*
- *Also, false criminal charges and disproportionate sentences have in some cases been used against persons seen as political enemies by those in power.*
- *The right to leave one's country (and also come back) has been much better established. The problem in some cases is rather that the door is closed on the receiving end.*
- *The rights of persons belonging to minorities continue to be badly respected. Racism, xenophobia, Islamophobia and rejection of Roma – as well as homophobia – are widespread in today's Europe.*
- *The enforced detention of dissidents in psychiatric institutions is no longer used as a major instrument of repression. However, there is still an urgent*

need to review policies depriving individuals of their legal capacity when regarded as mentally disabled.
– Prison conditions are still unsatisfactory all over Europe as a consequence of overcrowding and old, dilapidated prison buildings as well as political resistance against trying alternatives to imprisonment.
– The death penalty is de facto abolished in all Council of Europe countries. The moratorium has been prolonged in the Russian Federation. We are hoping for a total abolition.

In other words, the struggle has to continue. For our future endeavours I believe we have something to learn also from Sakharov's approach. Though the situation is now different, his ways and means remain relevant.

One aspect is the constant effort to be and appear to be constructive. While being uncompromisingly principled Sakharov was at the same time open-minded, striving always to understand the arguments on the other side. He believed in reason and the strength of the argument itself.

Even during his years in exile and through earlier periods of severe KGB harassment, he made constantly clear that he was seeking a rational dialogue. He sent numerous carefully drafted letters to the Soviet leaders seeking to convince them about the demands of reason, often referring to provisions in the law.

This was not reflection of simple naiveté; I have understood it to be part of a conscious approach. Of course, there was hardly any reply but the letters became known through informal channels and also reached abroad – and built a case. This is how Sakharov himself evaluated these efforts in his Memoirs:

> [They] have produced little in the way of immediate results. But I believe that statements on public issues are a useful means of promoting discussion, proposing alternatives to official policy, and focusing attention on problems. Appeals on behalf of specific individuals also attract attention to their cases, occasionally benefit a particular person, and inhibit future human rights violations through the threat of public disclosure.

Another aspect was his solidarity and empathy with victims. When his appeals went unheard he became more and more involved in non-violent, direct action, sometimes putting his own health at risk. He and his wife, Elena Bonner, acted upon a growing number of appeals from people who had been victimised by repression.

He travelled long distances to monitor trials and, when turned away from the court room, he demonstrated outside. He went on hunger strike several times, the first time in 1974 for the release of political prisoners.

When writing Reflections he prefaced the text with an epigraph from Goethe's Faust:

> He alone is worthy of life and freedom
> Who each day does battle for them anew!

He did himself point out the element of heroic romanticism in these lines, but in fact he demanded no less from himself than this daily battle. I assume the message to us is that human rights are at risk if not protected and defended. Human rights are not given; they have to be conquered again and again.

He gave us the broader arguments as to why this struggle is so important. Beyond compassion for fellow individuals, the protection of human rights is crucial for peace between peoples and for genuine development.

In his Nobel lecture in 1975, he argued that human rights are necessary to ensure democratic supervision of a country's foreign and security policy which would prevent militarisation and limit the risk of war. Also, human rights promote exchanges of information and ideas between people which in turn lowers the level of distrust and thereby the risk of conflict.

> I am convinced that international confidence, mutual understanding, disarmament and international security are inconceivable without an open society with freedom of information, freedom of conscience, the right to publish, and the right to travel and choose the country in which one wishes to live.

> *I am likewise convinced that freedom of conscience, together with the other civil rights, provides the basis for scientific progress and constitutes a guarantee that scientific advances will not be used to despoil mankind, providing the basis for economic and social progress, which in turn is a political guarantee for the possibility of an effective defence of social rights.*
>
> *At the same time I should like to defend the thesis of the original and decisive significance of civil and political rights in moulding the destiny of mankind.*

Sakharov was a true internationalist. He believed that the fates of all human beings are indivisible. "Mankind can develop painlessly only if it looks upon itself in a demographic sense as a unit, a single family without divisions into nations other than in matters of history and traditions," he wrote in Reflections.

This understanding of global interdependence made him express concern about human rights violations in Vietnam, Afghanistan, the Middle East and other parts of the world. Again, his interventions were principled, based on fact, free of any stereotyping and well argued.

The example and thoughts of Andrei Sakharov remain acutely relevant in today's world.

Thomas Hammarberg, 2009

Appendix 1

Andrei Sakharov – A chronology

1921 Andrei Dmitrievich Sakharov is born in Moscow on 21 May, the first child of Dmitri Sakharov and Ekaterina Sofiano.

1938 Matriculates in Physics Department, Moscow State University.

1941 *22 June: Germany invades the Soviet Union.*
July: Sakharov fails army medical exam because of chronic heart condition.
October: The Physics Department and Sakharov transferred to Ashkhabad.

1942 Sakharov graduates with honours. He works at an armament factory in Ulyanovsk from September 1942 until January 1945.

1943 10 July: Sakharov marries Klavdia Vikhireva. They have three children: Tatyana 1945; Lyubov 1949; Dmitri 1957.
Spring: Soviet project to build an atom bomb initiated under the direction of Igor Kurchatov.

1945 January: Sakharov accepted by Igor Tamm as a graduate student at the Theoretical Department of Moscow's Lebedev Physics Institute (FIAN).
May: Germany surrenders.
August: The United States drops atom bombs on Hiroshima and Nagasaki. Japan surrenders.

1947 Sakharov awarded Candidate of Science degree after defence of his thesis "Theory of 0-0 nuclear transitions."

1948 Sakharov included in Tamm's research group assigned to develop a thermonuclear (fusion) bomb.

1949 *First Soviet atom (fission) bomb tested on 29 August.*

1950 Sakharov transferred in March to Arzamas-16, the secret facility for the development of nuclear weapons, located at Sarov, near Gorky.

1950 Sakharov and Tamm develop the idea of realising a controlled thermonuclear reaction by magnetic confinement of a high-temperature plasma.

1952 *First US thermonuclear "super" device (too large to be used as a bomb) tested on 1 November 1952.*

1953 *5 March: Stalin dies.*
June: Sakharov awarded Doctor of Science degree.
12 August: The first Soviet thermonuclear bomb successfully tested. Sakharov was a principal author of its "layer cake" design, more powerful than the 1951 US "boosted" bomb.
October: Sakharov elected a full member of the USSR Academy of Sciences. Subsequently receives first Hero of Socialist Labour award and Stalin Prize.

1954 *The US tests a deliverable thermonuclear "super" bomb on 1 March.*

1955 22 November: The Soviet Union tests a thermonuclear "super" bomb. Sakharov is primary author of "the third idea," using the radiation of a fission bomb to trigger the fusion reaction.

1956 Sakharov receives second Hero of Socialist Labour Award and Lenin Prize.

1958 Sakharov publishes two articles on the danger of nuclear weapons tests: "Radioactive carbon in nuclear explosions and non-threshold biological effects" and a popular version, "Radiation danger of nuclear tests."

1961 Sakharov opposes the decision to resume nuclear weapons tests (the USSR, USA, and Great Britain had abstained from testing in 1959, 1960, and the first six months of 1961) and is reprimanded by Khrushchev.

1962 Khrushchev personally presents Sakharov with his third Hero of Socialist Labour Award.

1963 Sakharov campaigns to ban all nuclear tests except those conducted underground.
5 August: the Treaty Banning Nuclear Weapons Tests in the Atmosphere, in Outer Space, and Under Water is signed in Moscow.

1964 June: Sakharov successfully opposes Nikolai Nuzhdin's election to full membership in the Academy of Sciences on the grounds that he is a supporter of Lysenko's rejection of modern genetics.
October: Brezhnev replaces Khrushchev as General Secretary of the Communist Party.

1965 Arrest of writers Andrei Sinyavsky and Yuli Daniel for unauthorised publications in West.
5 December: First Pushkin Square Demonstration by Moscow human rights activists.

1966 Sakharov signs appeals against possible rehabilitation of Stalin and against introduction of new articles in the Criminal Code further restricting freedom of expression.
Attends Pushkin Square Demonstration for the first time.

1967 Joins Committee to Save Lake Baikal.
Writes letter to Brezhnev in defence of dissidents Ginzburg and Galanskov, and as a result, loses his post as a department head at Arzamas-16, but remains deputy scientific director.
Publishes a pioneering paper on the baryon asymmetry of the universe.

1968 Sakharov writes "Reflections on progress, co-existence and intellectual freedom". Publication of this essay in 40 foreign editions results in Sakharov's worldwide celebrity but also loss of his security clearance and his job in the Soviet weapons program.
21 August: Soviet troops occupy Czechoslovakia and end "Prague Spring."

1969 8 March: Sakharov's wife, Klavdia, dies of cancer.
May: Returns to Theoretical Department of FIAN as a senior scientist.
August. Donates his savings to charity.

1970 March: Writes, together with Valentin Turchin and Roy Medvedev, a letter to the Central Committee calling for democratisation of the Soviet Union.
October: Attends his first political trial of Revolt Pimenov and Boris Vail.
November: Co-founder, together with Valery Chalidze and Andrei Tverdokhlebov, of the Moscow Human Rights Committee.
December: Appeals for commutation of death penalty of Edward Kuznetsov and Mark Dymshits, convicted of attempting to hijack a plane and leave the USSR en route to Israel. While attending their appeal hearing, Sakharov becomes friendly with Elena Bonner.
Publishes "A multi-sheet cosmological model."

1971 March: Writes a memorandum to Brezhnev on domestic and foreign issues.
October: Sends open letter to the Supreme Soviet on the right to emigrate.

1972 7 January: Sakharov and Elena Bonner marry.
Sakharov drafts, collects signatures and submits to Supreme Soviet appeals for an amnesty for political prisoners and for abolition of the death penalty.
First interview (*Newsweek*, 8 November) published in western press.

1973 2 July: Broadcast of Sakharov's interview with Swedish correspondent Stenholm on Soviet problems sparks a warning from procurator and fierce attacks in the Soviet press.
September: Asks U.S. Congress to support Jackson Amendment linking trade benefits to the Soviet Union's emigration policy.

1974 May: Sakharov writes futurological article "The world in fifty years."
June: Six-day hunger strike to publicise plight of political prisoners.
Publishes "The scalar-tensor theory of gravitation."

1975 Sakharov writes "My country and the world".
1 August: The Final Act of the Conference on Security and Co-operation in Europe signed in Helsinki.
10 December: Receives the Nobel Peace Prize for "his struggle for human rights, for disarmament, and for co-operation between all nations." In Oslo Bonner reads his Nobel lecture "Peace, progress, and human rights" while Sakharov is in Vilnius attempting to attend the trial of Sergei Kovalev.

1976 April: Sakharov attends international conference on elementary particles in Tbilisi.
Sends appeal to Amnesty International calling for an amnesty for political prisoners throughout the world.
May: The Moscow Helsinki Watch Group founded.

1977 21 January: Sakharov writes to President Carter urging him to defend human rights activists. Carter replies on 5 February that "Human rights are a central concern of my administration."
25 January: Sakharov is officially warned by procurator that he is guilty of criminal slander of the KGB.
Sakharov writes "Alarm and hope" on the relations between the Soviet Union and the West.
Letter to Amnesty International on abolition of death penalty.

1978 May: Sakharov briefly detained by police after scuffle outside courthouse where Yuri Orlov is on trial.
Sakharov writes "The human rights movement in the USSR and Eastern Europe: Its goals, significance, and difficulties."
Begins writing his "Memoirs".

1979 Sakharov appeals on behalf of Crimean Tatars.
December: Soviet troops invade Afghanistan.

1980 January: Sakharov gives several interviews condemning Soviet invasion of Afghanistan and recommends boycott of 1980 Moscow Olympics unless troops are withdrawn.

22 January: Sakharov exiled by administrative order to Gorky for an indefinite term and deprived of his decorations for "systematic actions discrediting him as a recipient of State awards.
The US Congress and the European Parliament protest Sakharov's exile.
May: Writes "A letter from exile" on international and internal Soviet problems.
Two articles on elementary particles and one on cosmology are published.

1981 Sakharov writes "The responsibility of scientists."
22 November: Begins 17-day hunger strike which secures permission for Liza Alexeyeva to join Alexey Semyonov, her husband and Sakharov's stepson, in the US.

1982 August: Sakharov writes letter to 32nd Pugwash Conference on international security.
10 November: Brezhnev dies and is succeeded by Yuri Andropov as General Secretary.

1983 Sakharov's article "The danger of thermonuclear war" published in *Foreign Affairs*.
April: Sakharov receives the Szilard Award.

1984 *9 February: Andropov dies and is succeeded by Konstantin Chernenko as General Secretary.*
2 May: Bonner is arrested and on 10 August sentenced to five years' exile in Gorky for "slandering the Soviet system".
May: Sakharov begins a series of hunger strikes seeking permission for Bonner to travel to the USA for medical treatment.

1985 *10 March: Chernenko dies and is succeeded by Mikhail Gorbachev as General Secretary.*
October: Bonner receives permission to travel to the USA and Sakharov ends hunger strike.

1986 14 January: Bonner undergoes successful bypass surgery at Massachusetts General Hospital.
February: Sakharov appeals to Gorbachev calling for the release of prisoners of conscience.
26 April: The catastrophic meltdown of the Chernobyl nuclear reactor.
1 December: Writes Guri Marchuk, president of Academy of Sciences, letter on nuclear reactor safety and on the reduction of earthquake damage.
16 December: Gorbachev calls Sakharov and invites him to return to Moscow and "resume his patriotic work."
23 December: Sakharov and Bonner return to Moscow.
Sakharov returns to the Theoretical Department of FIAN.

1987 January: Sakharov sends another letter to Gorbachev urging an unconditional amnesty for political prisoners.
February: At the Moscow Forum for a Nuclear-Free World and the Survival of Mankind, Sakharov argues for liberalisation of the USSR and against Soviet linkage of nuclear weapons reduction to termination of US Strategic Defence Initiative.
Elected a director of the International Foundation for the Survival and Development of Mankind.
Appointed Chairman of the Academy of Sciences' Commission on Cosmomicrophysics.
Meets in Moscow with Margaret Thatcher, Jacques Chirac, Henry Kissinger, Cyrus Vance, Stephen Hawking, Jerome Wiesner, and other notables.
December: "The breakthrough must be continued and widened," an interview with Sakharov in which he proposes cutting the length of military service in half, is published in *Moscow News*.

1988 June: Sakharov's article "The inevitability of *perestroika*" published in the book *Inogo ne dano* (No other way).

August: Co-founder of the Moscow Tribune, a discussion club of the liberal intelligentsia.

August: Elected a member of the Memorial Society's Governing Council.

October: Participates in a Pugwash conference held in Dagomys.

October: Elected a member of the Presidium of the Academy of Sciences.

November: First foreign trip to attend a Board meeting of the International Foundation in Washington D.C., meets with President Reagan, Prime Minister Margaret Thatcher, President-elect Bush, Secretary of State Shultz, Senator Kennedy and Edward Teller.

December: Visits Paris to attend celebration of 40th anniversary of the Universal Declaration of Human Rights. Meets with President Mitterrand, Lech Walesa, and United Nations Secretary-General Javier Pérez de Cuéllar.

December: Visits Azerbaijan and Armenia in an attempt to resolve their conflict over Nagorno-Karabakh.

1989 April: Sakharov elected to the Congress of People's Deputies by the Academy of Sciences.

May: Visits Tbilisi to investigate the 9 April clash when Soviet troops attacked Georgian demonstrators and killed 21 persons.

25 May to 9 June: Speaks 12 times at the First Congress of People's Deputies and on the final day urges the repeal of Article 6 of the constitution, which served as the basis for the Communist Party's monopoly of power, and the transfer of final legislative authority to the Congress. Appointed to the Commission to Draft a New Constitution.

July: Elected a co-chair of the liberal Interregional Group of People's Deputies.

27 September: Delivers speech "On science and liberty" at the Congress of French Physicists in Lyon.

December: Calls for a two-hour general strike on 11 December to demonstrate support for quickening of *perestroika* and repeal of Article 6.

12 December: Attends the opening of the Second Congress of People's Deputies and is rebuked by Gorbachev and voted down by the Congress when he urges the abolition of Article 6.

14 December: Completes his draft Constitution of the Union of Soviet Republics of Europe and Asia. Attends caucus of the Interregional Group and urges that it function as a responsible political opposition.

14 December: Dies suddenly of a heart attack.

18 December: After four days of public mourning and funeral services attended by tens of thousands of Soviet citizens, Sakharov is buried in Moscow's Vostryakovskoe Cemetery.

1990 Sakharov's *Memoirs* are published in Russian, English, French, German, Italian, Polish, Japanese, Dutch, and other languages.

Appendix 2

Bibliography

Progress, Co-existence, and Intellectual Freedom, 1968
> Published by W.W. Norton in the United States and by Andrei Deutsch in the United Kingdom.

Sakharov Speaks, 1974
> Published in the United States by Alfred A. Knopf (ISBN 0-394-71302-8). Collection of Andrei Sakharov's essays, statements and appeals edited by Harrison Salisbury.

My Country and the World, 1975
> Published in the United States by Alfred A. Knopf (ISBN 0-394-72067-9).

Alarm and Hope, 1979
> Published by Alfred A. Knopf (ISBN 0-394-72743-7). Collection of Sakharov's public statements edited by Efrem Yankelevich and Alfred Friendly.

On Sakharov, 1982
> Published in the United States by Alfred A. Knopf (ISBN 0-394-72743-7). This Festschrift, containing articles by and about Sakharov, was edited by Alexander Babyonyshev for Sakharov's 60th birthday.

Andrei Sakharov and Peace, 1985
> Published in the United States by Avon Books. Anthology of articles by and about Andrei Sakharov, edited by Edward Lozansky.

Memoirs, 1990
> Published in the United States by Alfred A. Knopf (ISBN 0-394-53740-8). The *Memoirs* tell of the life of Andrei Sakharov up to his return from exile in December 1986. The *Bibliography, Glossary, and Index* included in the *Memoirs* are a useful reference tool on Sakharov and the Russian human rights movement.

Moscow and Beyond (1986-1989), 1990
> Published in the United States by Alfred A. Knopf (ISBN 0-394-58797-9). This book is a continuation of the *Memoirs*. It tells about crucial years of transformation of Soviet society.

Sales agents for publications of the Council of Europe
Agents de vente des publications du Conseil de l'Europe

BELGIUM/BELGIQUE
La Librairie Européenne -
The European Bookshop
Rue de l'Orme, 1
BE-1040 BRUXELLES
Tel.: +32 (0)2 231 04 35
Fax: +32 (0)2 735 08 60
E-mail: order@libeurop.be
http://www.libeurop.be

Jean De Lannoy/DL Services
Avenue du Roi 202 Koningslaan
BE-1190 BRUXELLES
Tel.: +32 (0)2 538 43 08
Fax: +32 (0)2 538 08 41
E-mail: jean.de.lannoy@dl-servi.com
http://www.jean-de-lannoy.be

**BOSNIA AND HERZEGOVINA/
BOSNIE-HERZÉGOVINE**
Robert's Plus d.o.o.
Marka Maruliça 2/V
BA-71000, SARAJEVO
Tel.: + 387 33 640 818
Fax: + 387 33 640 818
E-mail: robertsplus@bih.net.ba

CANADA
Renouf Publishing Co. Ltd.
1-5369 Canotek Road
CA-OTTAWA, Ontario K1J 9J3
Tel.: +1 613 745 2665
Fax: +1 613 745 7660
Toll-Free Tel.: (866) 767-6766
E-mail: order.dept@renoufbooks.com
http://www.renoufbooks.com

CROATIA/CROATIE
Robert's Plus d.o.o.
Marasoviçeva 67
HR-21000, SPLIT
Tel.: + 385 21 315 800, 801, 802, 803
Fax: + 385 21 315 804
E-mail: robertsplus@robertsplus.hr

**CZECH REPUBLIC/
RÉPUBLIQUE TCHÈQUE**
Suweco CZ, s.r.o.
Klecakova 347
CZ-180 21 PRAHA 9
Tel.: +420 2 424 59 204
Fax: +420 2 848 21 646
E-mail: import@suweco.cz
http://www.suweco.cz

DENMARK/DANEMARK
GAD
Vimmelskaftet 32
DK-1161 KØBENHAVN K
Tel.: +45 77 66 60 00
Fax: +45 77 66 60 01
E-mail: gad@gad.dk
http://www.gad.dk

FINLAND/FINLANDE
Akateeminen Kirjakauppa
PO Box 128
Keskuskatu 1
FI-00100 HELSINKI
Tel.: +358 (0)9 121 4430
Fax: +358 (0)9 121 4242
E-mail: akatilaus@akateeminen.com
http://www.akateeminen.com

FRANCE
La Documentation française
(diffusion/distribution France entière)
124, rue Henri Barbusse
FR-93308 AUBERVILLIERS CEDEX
Tél.: +33 (0)1 40 15 70 00
Fax: +33 (0)1 40 15 68 00
E-mail: commande@ladocumentationfrancaise.fr
http://www.ladocumentationfrancaise.fr

Librairie Kléber
1 rue des Francs Bourgeois
FR-67000 STRASBOURG
Tel.: +33 (0)3 88 15 78 88
Fax: +33 (0)3 88 15 78 80
E-mail: librairie-kleber@coe.int
http://www.librairie-kleber.com

**GERMANY/ALLEMAGNE
AUSTRIA/AUTRICHE**
UNO Verlag GmbH
August-Bebel-Allee 6
DE-53175 BONN
Tel.: +49 (0)228 94 90 20
Fax: +49 (0)228 94 90 222
E-mail: bestellung@uno-verlag.de
http://www.uno-verlag.de

GREECE/GRÈCE
Librairie Kauffmann s.a.
Stadiou 28
GR-105 64 ATHINAI
Tel.: +30 210 32 55 321
Fax.: +30 210 32 30 320
E-mail: ord@otenet.gr
http://www.kauffmann.gr

HUNGARY/HONGRIE
Euro Info Service
Pannónia u. 58.
PF. 1039
HU-1136 BUDAPEST
Tel.: +36 1 329 2170
Fax: +36 1 349 2053
E-mail: euroinfo@euroinfo.hu
http://www.euroinfo.hu

ITALY/ITALIE
Licosa SpA
Via Duca di Calabria, 1/1
IT-50125 FIRENZE
Tel.: +39 0556 483215
Fax: +39 0556 41257
E-mail: licosa@licosa.com
http://www.licosa.com

MEXICO/MEXIQUE
Mundi-Prensa México, S.A. De C.V.
Río Pánuco, 141 Delegacíon Cuauhtémoc
MX-06500 MÉXICO, D.F.
Tel.: +52 (01)55 55 33 56 58
Fax: +52 (01)55 55 14 67 99
E-mail: mundiprensa@mundiprensa.com.mx
http://www.mundiprensa.com.mx

NETHERLANDS/PAYS-BAS
Roodveldt Import BV
Nieuwe Hemweg 50
NL-1013 CX AMSTERDAM
Tel.: + 31 20 622 8035
Fax.: + 31 20 625 5493
Website: www.publidis.org
Email: orders@publidis.org

NORWAY/NORVÈGE
Akademika
Postboks 84 Blindern
NO-0314 OSLO
Tel.: +47 2 218 8100
Fax: +47 2 218 8103
E-mail: support@akademika.no
http://www.akademika.no

POLAND/POLOGNE
Ars Polona JSC
25 Obroncow Street
PL-03-933 WARSZAWA
Tel.: +48 (0)22 509 86 00
Fax: +48 (0)22 509 86 10
E-mail: arspolona@arspolona.com.pl
http://www.arspolona.com.pl

PORTUGAL
Livraria Portugal
(Dias & Andrade, Lda.)
Rua do Carmo, 70
PT-1200-094 LISBOA
Tel.: +351 21 347 42 82 / 85
Fax: +351 21 347 02 64
E-mail: info@livrariaportugal.pt
http://www.livrariaportugal.pt

**RUSSIAN FEDERATION/
FÉDÉRATION DE RUSSIE**
Ves Mir
17b, Butlerova.ul.
RU-117342 MOSCOW
Tel.: +7 495 739 0971
Fax: +7 495 739 0971
E-mail: orders@vesmirbooks.ru
http://www.vesmirbooks.ru

SPAIN/ESPAGNE
Mundi-Prensa Libros, s.a.
Castelló, 37
ES-28001 MADRID
Tel.: +34 914 36 37 00
Fax: +34 915 75 39 98
E-mail: libreria@mundiprensa.es
http://www.mundiprensa.com

SWITZERLAND/SUISSE
Planetis Sàrl
16 chemin des pins
CH-1273 ARZIER
Tel.: +41 22 366 51 77
Fax: +41 22 366 51 78
E-mail: info@planetis.ch

UNITED KINGDOM/ROYAUME-UNI
The Stationery Office Ltd
PO Box 29
GB-NORWICH NR3 1GN
Tel.: +44 (0)870 600 5522
Fax: +44 (0)870 600 5533
E-mail: book.enquiries@tso.co.uk
http://www.tsoshop.co.uk

**UNITED STATES and CANADA/
ÉTATS-UNIS et CANADA**
Manhattan Publishing Company
468 Albany Post Road
US-CROTON-ON-HUDSON, NY 10520
Tel.: +1 914 271 5194
Fax: +1 914 271 5856
E-mail: Info@manhattanpublishing.com
http://www.manhattanpublishing.com

Council of Europe Publishing/Editions du Conseil de l'Europe
FR-67075 STRASBOURG Cedex
Tel.: +33 (0)3 88 41 25 81 – Fax: +33 (0)3 88 41 39 10 – E-mail: publishing@coe.int – Website: http://book.coe.int